History and Existential Theology

HISTORY AND EXISTENTIAL THEOLOGY

The Role of History in the Thought of Rudolf Bultmann

by

Norman J. Young

The Westminster Press

Philadelphia

STANDARD BOOK NO. 664-20858-4
LIBRARY OF CONGRESS CATALOG CARD NO. 69-16303

PUBLISHED BY THE WESTMINSTER PRESS®
PHILADELPHIA, PENNSYLVANIA

PRINTED IN THE UNITED STATES OF AMERICA

To my wife, Barbara,
who made the endeavor
both possible and worthwhile

PREFACE

Although Karl Barth once predicted, probably with little enthusiasm, that the theological scene in the second half of the twentieth century would belong to Bultmann, there are signs that the post-Bultmannian era has already begun. I think that it has begun too soon, before the full dimensions of Bultmann's contribution to theology have been explored.

There are a number of reasons for this situation, among them being that too much attention has been given to one aspect of Bultmann's work, namely, the demythologizing project, and not enough to the wider implications of his views for understanding the Bible and reinterpreting doctrine. Another reason is that we have been encouraged to go beyond Bultmann, or to bypass him altogether, by the persistent but, I think, erroneous assertion that there is a fundamental inconsistency in his system, a contradiction between the existentialist interpretation of the faith that he calls for and his own continuing emphasis on God's saving act in Jesus Christ.

The main purpose of this book is to take another look at Bultmann's work, this time from a standpoint which he, his critics, and his followers all acknowledge to be important, namely, his view of history. I believe that an examination of his view of history provides a valuable perspective from which to understand not only his demythologizing project but the whole sweep of his Biblical interpretation. It also gives a basis for evaluating the criticisms that are commonly made of him, for tracing some of the so-called post-Bultmannian developments, and for seeing significant implications in his views for a reinterpretation of doctrine.

I am grateful for permission to reproduce, in amended form,

material from articles previously written and published in the following journals: *Australian Biblical Review*, Vol. 14, Dec. 1966 ("Some Aspects of Bultmann's Hermeneutics"); *Church Quarterly Review*, Vol. 165, 1964 ("Bultmann's View of History"); *Scottish Journal of Theology*, Vol. 19, Sept. 1966 ("Bultmann's View of the Old Testament").

I am also indebted, in the section on the Old Testament, to discussions in a seminar on Old Testament typology led by Dr. Bernhard Anderson at Drew University in 1958, and to some draft translations circulated in that seminar.

My thanks are due to a great many people. To my friend and teacher Carl Michalson, who first introduced me to Bultmann's thought; to another friend and teacher, Will Herberg, who has helped me to see the theological significance of various views of history; to the Australian Methodist Church and to Drew University for earlier opportunities for study; to President James McCord and Princeton Theological Seminary for the Fellowship and library facilities that made the final writing possible; and, by no means least, to my wife and sons who, far from merely tolerating my long-standing preoccupation with Bultmann, have actively encouraged me in the work.

N. J. Y.

Queens College
Melbourne, Australia

CONTENTS

Part III. History and Doctrine

Part I

BULTMANN'S VIEW OF HISTORY

1

INTRODUCTION: AN EXISTENTIALIST APPROACH

IT SEEMS ALMOST INEVITABLE that any attempt to describe Bultmann's approach to history will make use of the label "existentialist." This is unfortunate in a way, because while there is some truth in saying that Bultmann takes an existentialist view of history, this really tells us very little. In the first place, the label is used with such abandon these days that it is difficult to know in any given case what it is supposed to mean. As Carl Michalson once said, the term may apply "all the way from styles in hats to the most serious technical philosophies. One may know of it chiefly from the cabarets he has visited, or one may know of it from his tilts with learned journals."[1] So, to say that Bultmann's approach to history is an existentialist one is not particularly instructive. Nor is it really accurate, because some of the ideas about history that Bultmann accepts and that earn for him the existentialist tag are shared by many who are not usually called existentialists at all. The key components in this approach are simply the recognition that man stands within the stream of historical happening, and the realization that this fact has implications for apprehending the meaning of history. Obviously this recognition is by no means the prerogative of existentialists, and Gogarten is right when he refers to this approach simply as "modern historical method," crediting Dilthey with making this understanding of history explicit in the modern era.[2]

On looking more closely at this approach which Bultmann follows, we see three main features. First is his insistence, almost universally accepted, that history is not merely an aggregation of uninterpreted happenings. History is not, as Henry Ford is reputed to have claimed, "one dam' thing after another"; or, in

Bultmann's less graphic terms, history is not properly understood when it is seen only "as a field of such events and actions as can be fixed in space and time."[3] What needs to be added? Bultmann answers by making the point that is fundamental to his whole system, that a "historical event or action as historical includes its meaning or importance."[4]

This brings us to the question of how to find the meaning of a historical event, which is the second feature of Bultmann's approach. Negatively, Bultmann denies that meaning can be found by observation from some vantage point outside history. Man lacks, as he puts it, the Archimedean point.[5] An airplane flies above the ground, and its passengers see a pattern of land and sea, cities and forests and roads. They can see where they have come from even after takeoff, and can see where they are going before they land. But man cannot get above history in that way. The overall pattern does not become clear, because memory gives a blurred and fragmentary picture of the past and anticipation gives an unreliable picture of the future. We can find no answer to the question of the meaning of history as a whole. So Bultmann says:

> It must be understood that the quest for meaning in history cannot find an answer if we ask for the meaning of history in its totality. If man is to achieve this, the meaning in history, he must have a stand outside history from which he can look at history, or he must take his stand at the goal of history from where he can look back into past history. But no philosopher or historian stands outside history or at its goal. They all stand within history and are historical.[6]

How, then, is meaning to be found? On the positive side, Bultmann insists that the historian should begin with what is acknowledged to be the core of history—man himself. Meaning in history is to be found not as man looks around himself and into the maelstrom of universal history, seeking order in the chaos of past and present events, but only as he begins with his own personal history. This immediately narrows the field and gives a point of reference from which to begin to understand events of world history. He seeks to understand *himself* in relation to these events. However, this understanding is not that of an onlooker, nor of one who is entirely at the mercy of the so-called "forces of history," for while his possibilities are dictated to him by the past, he is still able to decide between these possibilities. In these decisions he constitutes his own personal history. We could say that man does not *find* meaning in history at all in the sense of discovering ready-made the significance of the situation into which the vagaries of history have led him. Instead, he *makes* meaning as he decides how to understand himself and how to act in the light of what has happened to him. "Always in your present lies the meaning of history," says Bultmann, "and you cannot see it as a spectator, but you can realize it in your responsible decisions."[7]

This link between self-understanding and understanding of history may be seen more clearly by relating it to an illustration that R. G. Collingwood was fond of using. Collingwood contends that to understand history is to think other people's thoughts after them.[8] He cites the incident during the battle of Trafalgar when Nelson's subordinates, afraid that he would become the prime target of enemy snipers if recognized, asked him to cover the insignia that would identify him. He refused and said: "In honor I gained them, and in honor I will die with them." Collingwood enlarges on this, claiming that we can understand this historical event adequately only if we can think ourselves back into Nelson's position and can imagine what it was like to be on the deck of the *Victory* under enemy fire. Bultmann would go farther than this. In his view we can understand the event and Nelson's statement not just when we think ourselves back into his situation but when we are in the same kind of situation ourselves, facing the same decision whether to hide our identity or not in the face of danger. Under these circumstances, to understand Nelson is at the same time to understand ourselves, and this understanding is actually constituted[9] in the decision that we make when confronted with a parallel decision. In a university college that I know very well the undergraduates engage in a fireworks battle every November 5, so the Master of the College faces annually the decision whether to attempt to put a stop to the fray by appearing in the thick of it and identifying himself or to avoid bombardment by remaining incognito under the cover of darkness. Therefore, according to Bultmann, no one is in a better position to understand the Trafalgar incident and Nelson's decision than the Master of the College!

The third characteristic feature of this approach to history is really a corollary. If meaning is to be found in the way just described, then the purpose of doing history, that is, of engaging in historical research, should be not just to reconstruct past happenings but to interpret them in such a way that they impinge upon our present self-understanding. Therefore, historical method must see the question of human existence as primary and must approach its material with this foremost in mind.

This general approach can now be summarized. It is based upon the recognition that man is the central figure in history and that he cannot extricate himself from it. Therefore, meaning is to be found not in the totality of history but in the personal history of each man himself. This personal history does not just unfold before us but is shaped by our own responsible decisions. Consequently, a proper approach to history must have the question of human existence as primary and must look for meaning in the dimension of the personal and the present.

As soon as this kind of summary is given, of course the questions begin. Perhaps meaning is to be found in the present, but is not history really concerned with the past? Is not history immeasurably reduced and distorted by making self the key? When we decide ahead of time that the primary question to bring to history is that of human existence, have we not already preshaped the answer? How can understanding of the self in history be separated from or given precedence over the history of nations and the world? And once this understanding of history is applied to traditional assertions about Christian faith another barrage of questions begins. What does it now mean to say that Christianity is rooted in history? In what sense is Christianity based on an act of God in history? Does not the gospel point away from ourselves and our own history toward God and his acts? Do Christian doctrines come to focus in God's acts or our self-understanding? Whatever may at this stage be obscure, at least it is clear that this kind of approach to history has a number of significant implications for hermeneutics, exegesis, theological method, and doctrinal formulations.[10] These implications will be developed and evaluated in Parts II and III, but before we come to that it is necessary to consider in more detail Bultmann's view of history, which so far has been dealt with only in general terms and in an introductory way.

2
THE STRUCTURE OF HISTORY

IN HIS *Primitive Christianity* and *History of the Synoptic Tradition,* Bultmann gives us the results of his own historical research. In his *History and Eschatology* he describes and evaluates the views of others, at the same time conveying something of his own attitude toward history, an attitude already reflected in his commentary on John and in his *Theology of the New Testament.* But in no one place does Bultmann set out consistently and in detail what his view of the structure of history is. This begins to emerge, however, as we consider the terms that he most commonly uses in relation to history, and the context in which they apply.

a. Natur *and* Geschichte

We should begin by recognizing the distinction that Bultmann draws between "nature" and "history." At first sight this seems straightforward enough. Nature is the realm of what could be called "natural phenomena," for example, the cycle of seasons, earthquakes, the life of animals, and so on. History, on the other hand, is the field of human actions. Obviously these are not entirely separate, because natural occurrences become part of history if men are involved and react to them. History is not cut off from nature, because the natural world is the context within which man lives. However, Bultmann insists that a distinction can be made between the two, and in fact must be made if we are properly to understand ourselves as historical beings. As early as 1926 he was contending that

> our relationship to history is wholly different from our relationship to nature. Man, if he rightly understands himself,

> differentiates himself from nature. When he observes nature, he perceives there something objective which is not himself. When he turns his attention to history, however, he must admit himself to be a part of history; he is considering a living complex of events in which he is essentially involved. . . . Hence there cannot be an impartial observation of history in the same sense that there can be an impersonal observation of nature.[1]

As recently as 1966 he was making the same point, although this time he was careful to explain that the distinction is phenomenological rather than metaphysical,[2] reflecting a difference of methodological approach rather than two ontologically separate realms. Natural science employs an objectifying method of research through which conclusions are reached by impartial observation and rigid calculation. The object of this type of inquiry can be called "nature" even when man himself may be part of the inquiry, for this method deals with him only as one natural phenomenon among many. On the other hand, the method of history is "subjective" in the sense that the historian is inextricably involved with his subject matter. The conclusions he draws are not external to the process being studied; they are decisions that are actually constitutive of history which is being apprehended and lived.

What Bultmann is suggesting here is not just that there are two overlapping areas, related but distinguishable by the different method of approach appropriate to each, but also that the method of approach somehow determines the status of what is being apprehended. So, for instance, he contends that the Greeks, by approaching the realm of human action with the objective method proper to nature, objectified what is normally the province of history into nature.[3] And conversely he says that because the Hebrews looked upon the world of nature as "the sphere of God's sovereignty and the stage for man's labors and the working out of his destiny," then in effect they regarded this as "history rather than nature."[4]

Bultmann makes very little of the point that what belongs primarily in the realm of nature may become history if a different method of approach is used. But he does make a great deal of the fact that what properly belongs to the realm of history because it has to do with the life of man may be approached objectively with the tools appropriate to nature. Sometimes, as we have just seen, Bultmann indicates that such an approach effects a transfer from the realm of history into that of nature, but usually he makes the same point by employing different terminology. When history is "objectivized" in this way, Bultmann labels both the approach and the events that are so approached as *historisch,* in contrast to *geschichtlich.* These two terms will be considered in more detail in the next section, but before we move to this, two or three further comments should be made about Bultmann's *Natur-Geschichte* distinction.

(i) As Heinrich Ott has shown,[5] this distinction is parallel to one frequently made by existentialist philosophers. He cites, for instance, Sartre's distinction between two ways of being, *en soi* and *pour soi;* and the contrast that Jaspers draws between objective and existential truth; and the different modes of being in the world, *Dasein* and *Vorhandensein,* which Heidegger points to. Ott does not mention the even closer parallel between Bultmann's distinction and Buber's primordial *I-It* and *I-Thou* relations. In both Buber and Bultmann it is not the object that determines the relation or approach, but the relationship itself is constitutive of the object. So, according to Buber, if I relate to another person as though he were something to be manipulated for my own ends, then in that *I-It* relationship he becomes a different person from the one to whom I might have related as a *Thou.* According to Bultmann, if man is studied objectively, with no account taken of his freedom, his self-understanding, or his decisions in concrete situations, then he becomes part of nature rather than of history.[6] In addition, both Buber and Bultmann go on to say that in these relationships the subject also is affected by the method of approach. Something happens to me if, in Buber's terminology, I begin to treat another as an *It* rather than as a *Thou;* or, to put it Bultmann's way, who a man is depends upon how he relates to others in history. If, for instance, certain past events become present reality as they are approached as part of history rather than nature, then these not only add to a man's store of factual knowledge, they become part of who he is.

(ii) The distinction between *Natur* and *Geschichte* as Bultmann draws it is so basic to his thought that serious misunderstandings arise if it is not properly recognized, as the following example shows. One of the charges most commonly leveled against Bultmann is that he removes the historical dimension from the Christian faith. When he protests that it never has been his intention to remove the connection between past history and present faith, his critics repeat the charge as though he had never replied, or as though his reply represents only a temporary and inconsistent change of heart and is therefore not to be taken seriously.[7] The reason for this impasse is that the very procedure many critics advocate as necessary in order to establish the historical basis for the Christian faith is one which, for Bultmann, effectively removes the inquiry from the historical realm. Bultmann does not deny that the past event of Jesus of Nazareth is indispensable to the Christian faith. In fact, he affirms this with an insistence that embarrasses some of his most ardent supporters.[8] Nor does he deny that objective-historical research into the life and teaching of Jesus can be fruitful.[9] But he does deny that any such approach can establish Jesus as the Christ, insisting that every such attempt removes the event from the historical realm and makes faith response, within which one's own being is constituted, impossible. This is not to say that Bultmann's estimate of the quest for the historical Jesus is necessarily valid. In fact, as I shall indicate later, I think it ought to be modified. However, it is clear that much of the criticism of Bultmann's alleged weakening of the historical basis of the Christian faith fails to take account of his nature-history distinction, and so is unable to take him seriously when he affirms the centrality of God's act in history in the event of Jesus Christ.[10]

(iii) While Bultmann is not reluctant to acknowledge his indebtedness to the insights of existentialist philosophers—Heidegger in particular—he sees the nature-history distinction reflected not only in their writings but, more importantly, in the difference between Greek and Biblical thought. For the former, nature was the dominant category. The meaning of the world and of human life was inherent in nature and its relationships, so that the view of history was obscured and the task of historiography downgraded. In this system, man becomes an object of investigation like any other natural object, and he is important only as an individual instance of a general rule.[11] In the Biblical view, however, history is the dominant category. God reveals himself in history rather than in nature, and man finds himself and his place not within nature as instance of a general rule but over against nature with a history given him by God:

> The real life of man, therefore, develops in the sphere of what is individual—of contingent encounter. . . . It is here in decision, and not in the upward flight of his thoughtful contemplation toward the timeless world of the divine, that he stands before God.[12]

Therefore, when Bultmann reinterprets traditional theological formulations, setting them within the context of present decision and encounter rather than in the realm of nature and the eternal, he sees this not as introducing alien existentialist thought forms into Biblical categories but as a reassertion of the genuinely historical, and therefore Biblical, dimension in place of a world view oriented toward nature.[13]

b. Historisch *and* geschichtlich

Within the realm of history (*Geschichte*) in the broad sense of "that which is constituted by human actions" there is a distinction that has already been anticipated and that now must be considered in more detail. In the German language, there are two terms in common use which can be translated "history," namely, *Historie* and *Geschichte*. In everyday usage they are interchangeable, although a more discriminating use reserves *Geschichte* for the historical reality (events, occurrences) while *Historie* refers to the study and description of *Geschichte*. However, it is also common knowledge that German theologians have used these terms to make a more sophisticated distinction, one that was made explicit by Julius Schniewind:

> In German theology we are familiar with the remarkable distinction between *Historie* and *Geschichte*. . . . *Geschichte* means the mutual encounter of persons, *Historie* the causal nexus in the affairs of men. The latter is the subject matter of historical science, which seeks to divest itself of all presuppositions and prejudices and to establish objective facts. *Geschichte*, on the other hand, cannot achieve such impartiality, for the encounter which it implies vitally affects our personal existence: it demands resolve and decision, yes or no, love or hate.[14]

Bultmann is presumably in agreement with this way of making the distinction, since he has no comment in his reply to Schniewind. However, this does not fully describe the structure of history as Bultmann sees it, because the vital and theologically relevant question of how these two realms are related remains unanswered. Actually, Bultmann hardly ever uses the term *Historie*, and then only according to common usage, unless he is replying to specific criticisms couched in the *Historie-Geschichte* terminology, in which case he replies in kind. So in order to be true to Bultmann's own thought and to avoid accusing him prematurely of making too radical a separation between dimensions of history, we should consider the terms that he usually chooses, namely, *historisch* and *geschichtlich*.

Although he is not completely consistent in his use of these terms,[15] the underlying distinction to which they usually point does remain constant. In the first place, the terms refer to two different methods of approach that may be made to history, history (*Geschichte*) here being understood in the broadest sense as the field of human actions. A *historisch* approach is one that would be appropriate in the field of natural science; i.e., its method is detached, observation is made from a neutral standpoint,[16] and the result evokes the past by giving factual information about it.[17] The *geschichtlich* approach, on the other hand, is involved rather than detached. It approaches the subject matter with the question of human existence as primary, thus precipitating existential encounter with the events of history. In this encounter the historian puts his own existence in question, presupposing that the main thrust of his work will be toward the present rather than the past. The main features of this *geschichtlich* approach have already been described in Chapter 1 as the existential or modern historical approach.

In the second place, these terms are used to distinguish the different types of event that result when history is approached in these different ways. When the area of human activity is viewed in a detached and objectivizing way, it is seen as a series of events unfolding in the course of time, understandable as a "chain of cause and effect."[18] An occurrence understood in this way Bultmann calls a *historisch* event. It is given its place among the phenomena of the *kosmos*,[19] and is capable of complete examination and description by objective historical research.[20] But when the approach is *geschichtlich* the constitutive elements of history are not merely past occurrences; they become present events within which one's own existence is disclosed.[21] This type of event Bultmann calls *geschichtlich*. To understand its meaning is at the same time to understand oneself in relation to it. Suppose, for instance, that the occurrence under consideration is the American Declaration of Independence.[22] The *historisch* approach would be that of the historian who notes the contents of the document, the signatories and their motives, the attendant circumstances, and so on. A *geschichtlich* approach would be that of an immigrant to the United States who, having read the document, is confronted with the decision whether to become a United States citizen and thus to make the Declaration part of his own historicity (*Geschichtlichkeit*).

This distinction is illustrated by Bultmann himself in a key passage in his essay "New Testament and Mythology," where it is clear that the distinction applies both to the methods of approach and to the resultant events:

> In so far as it is a saving event, the Cross of Christ is no mythical fact but is an historical event (*ein geschichtliche Geschehen*) which has its origin in the objective-historical

> fact (*in dem historischen Ereignis*) of the crucifixion of Jesus of Nazareth. This is historical in its significance as the judgment passed upon the world and the deliverance of man. It is in this sense that Christ is crucified "for us."[23]

From this we are able to see that for Bultmann the characteristics of the *historisch* event are its facticity (i.e., its having happened in the past at a time and place that can be located) and its being open to verification by objective research. On the other hand, the *geschichtlich* event is one that is present, having existential significance here and now for us, and for which there can be no verification apart from faithful participation in the event. It is clear that for Bultmann these are two different events. It is equally clear that he sees an indispensable connection between the two. What this connection is will be discussed in detail later, but a preliminary indication here will help to clarify the relation and the distinction between *historisch* and *geschichtlich.*

Bultmann is concerned to retain the connection between faith on the one hand and the cross of Christ as past event on the other, and he does this by insisting that while faith is response to the *geschichtlich* event, the event in the present, this present event has its origin in the unique happening in the past. The *historisch* occurrence becomes *geschichtlich* event as it is made contemporary and significant through preaching and sacrament, both of which Bultmann sees as personal encounter. Therefore, the connection between *historisch* occurrence and *geschichtlich* event is not that the former is reproduced in memory, or that the observer is somehow able to transport himself back into imagination into the past, but that the past event is renewed in such a way that it becomes of decisive significance for one's own existence in the present. This, Bultmann claims, is achieved in the kerygma. When the past event of the crucifixion (which can be located in space-time and is therefore *historisch,* open to objective historical research) is proclaimed as the cross that judges the world and puts my existence in jeopardy, then it becomes the *geschichtlich* event, the saving event.

It is at this point that Bultmann is consistently misunderstood by both critics and supporters. They claim that his view amounts to this—that as long as there is a *message* of salvation to which one may respond, then there is no need for the actual past-historical *occurrence* at all. But with equal consistency Bultmann has denied this implication, most recently in his reply to Macquarrie when he reiterates that "there is no existential interpretation of history at all which ignores the factual occurrence."[24] He does not regard the factual character of history and of Jesus as "in any way irrelevant for faith and for theology,"[25] for while faith is response to the *geschichtlich* event which occurs in the present, this has, as we have seen, the occurrence in the past as its necessary ground and origin. Of course it may be argued that Bultmann should not affirm this indissoluble link between the saving event in the present and the past event of Jesus of Nazareth, and the validity of this line of argument will be discussed later, but in the meantime it is important to recognize that for Bultmann the two go together, and, he believes, must go together if the integrity of the Christian kerygma is to be retained.

Heinrich Ott criticizes Bultmann's *historisch-geschichtlich* distinction, claiming that he has elevated a methodological distinction into an ontological one,[26] and has thereby hypostatized the data of empirical-objective research into a different realm from the subject matter of the existential approach. But Ott, in making the charge in the way that he does, acknowledges that for Bultmann it is the mode of apprehension, or better, the relationship in which meaning is found, that is primary; and while the realms are distinguished by Bultmann, they are also very closely connected. What Ott calls "hypostatization" is therefore better understood as an implication of the existential approach to history which holds that neither subject nor object remains the same when the relationship between them changes. So the event which includes a *historisch* apprehension is not the same as the one in which the apprehension is *geschichtlich*. Events of the former kind are said by Bultmann to belong to the dimension of *Weltgeschichte*, or "world history,"[27] while *geschichtlich* events are constitutive of *Geschichtlichkeit*, or personal history.

c. Geschichtlichkeit

We have been saying that a *geschichtlich* event, in contrast to a *historisch* event, is constituted in present encounter and comes to have decisive significance for human existence. This human existence insofar as it is constituted within these *geschichtlich* events Bultmann refers to as *Geschichtlichkeit*, "personal history" or "historicity." Since man is the central feature of history, *Geschichtlichkeit* is, for Bultmann, the focal point in the structure of history. But this does not mean simply that man is the most significant feature of world history, nor that historical writing is primarily concerned with man and his activity. This is true and is inevitable, since man occupies the central place in history, but it does not tell us *why* man occupies this place. What does Bultmann mean to convey by claiming that historicity is the focal feature of history?

We get a clue to his meaning from his acceptance of one aspect of the views of historical relativists and his rejection of another. He agrees that man must be viewed primarily as historical, so that what makes him "man" is not some suprahistorical essence but simply his inextricable involvement with historical events: "Man cannot choose the place from which he starts; it is given to him by the past. . . . The nature of man is 'historicity.' "[28] But he denies that man who is inextricably involved with these events is thereby determined by them. He is influenced but not defined by what happens in history. So Bultmann says:

> Historicism is perfectly right in seeing that every present situation grows out of the past; but it misunderstands the determination by the past as purely causal determination. . . . It does not understand the present situation as the situation of decision—a decision which, as our decision over against the future, is at the same time our decision over against the past concerning the way in which it is to determine the future.[29]

So Bultmann sees the situation of man within history as one both of givenness and of possibility. The past gives to man his place, but also gives him a range of possibilities for the future. He is therefore responsible in the present to decide from among these possibilities and thus to choose his future.

It is just this existence of man in the present with his givenness and his possibility that Bultmann means by *Geschichtlichkeit*, as we see in his own definition of the term:

> The historicity of the human being is completely understood when the human being is understood as living in responsibility over against the future, and therefore in decision. And, furthermore, it must be said that historicity in its fullest sense is not a self-evident natural quality of the human individual, but a possibility which must be grasped and realized.[30]

Therefore, to say that man is historical is not just to acknowledge that his existence is bound up with the course of world history. It is also to recognize that his existence is constituted within the framework of responsible decisions that he makes in the present by which "the yield of the past is gathered in and the meaning of the future is chosen."[31] It is just this responsible decision that constitutes his *Geschichtlichkeit* and so makes him a historical being.

It is not difficult now to see the break between Bultmann's view of man and that of the classical idealist. According to the latter, man is one who *has* a history, while Bultmann affirms that man *is* his history. In other words, the real life of man is not an integration into the life of the cosmos achieved because his essential being lifts him above the contingencies of history. Man is nothing other than what he becomes by virtue of his concrete encounters and decisions. Therefore, the *Geschichtlichkeit* of man must never be seen as his possession, nor as a quality or essence that he brings to his historical situation and which then determines the way he will act in that situation. *Geschichtlichkeit*, being the existence of man constituted in the moment of decision, looks forward to a future chosen in the present and not determined by the past.

Although Bultmann denies making a metaphysical distinction between two realms of history, insisting instead that he is simply distinguishing two approaches to history, there is no doubt that he views as preeminent the *geschichtlich* approach that concentrates on man's historicity. When he refers to man as the central feature of history, the implication is that any historiographical method is "truly historical" only as it seeks to elucidate one's own existence within history. It is not enough to come to history in order to study the phenomenon "man." This is not what Bultmann means by saying that man's *Geschichtlichkeit* is the central feature of history. He means that the genuinely historical approach seeks to understand one's own historicity by coming to terms with one's own situation within history and deciding in the light of this situation how to respond to the possibilities resident within it. This, Gogarten contends, is what is involved in the modern understanding of history:

> Modern man is able to envisage history only from the point of view of his own responsibility for it. . . . Surely precisely this is the grasping of the actual essential nature of history, or, as we may express it, of the historical character (*Geschichtlichkeit*) of human existence.[32]

So far in this analysis of the structure of history as Bultmann views it we have not seen anything that is distinctively Christian. Even the stress on personal historicity is, as Gogarten says, characteristic of modern rather than specifically Christian understanding of history. It is just here that Bultmann himself raises the question of the uniquely Christian dimension and gives a significant answer:

> What is the peculiarity of the Christian faith besides the fact that it understands the human being as historical? Christian faith believes that man does not have the freedom which is presupposed for historical decisions.[33]

In other words, man finds himself in a paradoxical situation. As a historical being he is faced with the responsibility of making decisions. In these decisions he actually constitutes himself, for in choosing his own future he shapes his personal history in the present. But in fact these decisions lose most of their authenticity because man is largely bound to his past understanding of himself. Out of his past, man has become what he is, and in the last resort he is unwilling to be rid of this past that is himself. In order to be free in the present and for the future he would have to break the binding force of the past. But this would be to get rid of himself, to become a "new man," and this, according to Christian faith, man is unable to achieve for himself. But according to Christian faith also, it is just this that is achieved in Christ and given to man as a gift. And precisely this, for Bultmann, is the meaning of the Christian claim that Jesus Christ is the eschatological event. He brings history to an end in the sense of ending a man's past history, his past understanding of himself, and grants to him the possibility for free decision and thus new and authentic existence.

So a new dimension in Bultmann's view of history appears. This is the aspect of *Geschichtlichkeit* that is constituted by man's faithful response in the light of the eschatological event. Bultmann refers to this as *eschatologische Existenz,* "eschatological existence."

d. Eschatologische Existenz

Just as the *Geschichtlichkeit* of man is constituted by decision in the light of *geschichtlich* events, so eschatological existence is the historicity of man as he is reconstituted in the light of the eschatological event. This event which places the believer in eschatological existence may take him away from the world,[34] or at least may grant him freedom so that his relationship to the world is dialectical,[35] but it does not remove him from history. Bultmann affirms that human life "continues to be 'historic' even when it is eschatological . . . and it issues forth in new life,"[36] and goes as far as saying that eschatological existence is human life in its real historicity.[37] Put this way, what Bultmann means by eschatological existence is far from clear. One of his critics has said that this sounds like a riddle: When is an event which is not historical still an event? Answer: when it is eschatological.[38] Although such a comment reflects more exasperation than illumination, Bultmann himself is partly to blame. Actually, he insists that the eschatological event is also historical, but what he means by eschatological, and how this fits into his overall view of history, certainly needs further elucidation.

Bultmann uses the term "eschatological" very often and in a variety of ways. In one essay, for instance,[39] he uses it of institutions (covenant, people of God), of divine activity, and of human life. Chaotic as this may at first appear, closer examination shows that there is a common feature that gives some warrant for using the same term in these different ways. In each case the term conveys the meaning of *transcending world history*. The covenant is eschatological because its realization is not to be sought within the world. The people of God is an eschatological community because it is not simply to be identified as a particular race or nation of the world. God's activity is eschatological because it is not identifiable as such by a *historisch* approach to world history. Man's existence is eschatological because its ground and fulfillment are found beyond this world. The Kingdom of God is eschatological in the same sense of transcending the order of world history.[40] Simply listed in this way, these references may seem to echo sheer supernaturalism or otherworldliness. They need to be heard against the background of Bultmann's view of the structure of history in which there are a number of dimensions, the focal one being that of *Geschichtlichkeit*. Then the term "eschatological" applied to events, institutions, or way of life indicates that these are visible in the world and have a point of reference in world history, but also have meaning that transcends this order, inhering primarily in the dimension of personal history.

Clearly enough Bultmann is not using the term "eschatological" in its usual sense. Traditionally the two defining references are to the future and to the end of world history. This implies a unilateral view of history in which the history that is brought to an end by the eschatological event is world history, and, with it, personal history, because the two are seen as coextensive. Since this has not yet happened, it follows that this must still be in the future. However, because Bultmann sees *Geschichtlich-*

keit as a dimension of history that transcends *Weltgeschichte*, he is able to speak of an event that brings to an end one dimension of history but not necessarily the other. For him the eschatological event occurs in the dimension of personal history, bringing to an end one's old self and opening the way to the new, but it does not at the same time bring world history to an end.

Does this then imply that the meaning of the term "eschatological" inheres in some special kind of personal existence quite unrelated to the ordinary events of the world? Not for Bultmann, for, as we have already seen, Bultmann sees personal history as constituted in existential response to the givenness of world history. Nor is the eschatological event some kind of mystical awareness that occurs solely in the mind or experience of an individual. For Bultmann, the eschatological event is inextricably linked to an occurrence in world history, namely, the past event of Jesus of Nazareth. When the significance of this event is proclaimed in the present so that one's own existence is at stake in the response that is made, then the eschatological event occurs:

> According to the New Testament Jesus Christ is the eschatological event, which means that he is the action of God by which he has set an end to the old world. In the preaching of the Christian Church the eschatological event will ever again become present and becomes present ever again. The old world has reached its end for him in so far as he himself as the old man has reached his end and is now a new man, a free man.[41]

So the history that comes to an end in the eschatological event is personal history, and the world that is renewed is the world of man's own existence. But although the eschatological event transcends the dimension of world history, there is clearly a relation between the two. It does not exist in some supernatural sphere removed from the realities of the world, to be apprehended by some rational essence of man that sets him apart from the vagaries of history. But neither does the eschatological event exist as an event of the past that can be identified as eschatological by a *historisch* inquiry. The eschatological event occurs only in the present as Christ is proclaimed and encountered in existential response. So Bultmann says:

> Christ is everything that is asserted of him in so far as he is the Eschatological Event. But he is not this in such a way that this would be expressible in terms of a world event. Yet neither is he this as an event in an exalted supernatural sphere, which indeed would be simply a "world" event. Jesus Christ cannot be objectively established as an Eschatological Event so that one could there and then believe in him. Rather he is such, or, to put it more exactly, he becomes such in the encounter, when the Word which proclaims him meets with belief: and indeed even when it does not meet with belief, for whoever does not believe is already judged.[42]

So, Bultmann asserts, God confronts man in an event which is at the same time historical and eschatological.[43]

Many more questions have been raised here about the meaning of Christ as the eschatological event than have been answered. To what extent, for instance, is the event which is God's saving action dependent upon human response? Should we not say of the past event that there and then God's saving purpose was fulfilled? Is it true, and is it consistent with Bultmann's other assertions that the event of Jesus of Nazareth and no other becomes eschatological? These and related questions will be discussed in Part III, where the doctrinal implications of Bultmann's view of history will be considered in more detail. Here we have been concerned to show how Bultmann's view of history enables him to speak of an event which, when called eschatological, refers to an ending and a new beginning of personal history rather than world history while still having an essential point of reference on the plane of world history.

As man encounters the eschatological event in the kerygma and responds in faith he enters into eschatological existence. The major features of such existence Bultmann describes variously as "freedom from the world," "detachment from the world," or "withdrawal from the world."[44] But this detachment is not an ascetic one, nor a mystical flight from the realm of history. It implies living within the world but preserving a distance, "dealing with it in a spirit of 'as if not.' "[45] Although man is given a new understanding of himself and is therefore no longer bound to the world as he was in the past, nevertheless the future for which he is now free is still his future as a historical being. It is, Bultmann claims, this very sense of detachment from the world that enables him to live responsibly within the world. It is just because he realizes that his destiny is not finally determined by the world and its structures that he is able to live responsibly within these, speaking critically and acting for reformation when necessary. It is just because he knows that this world is not ultimately meaningful in itself but makes sense only in the context of a God who transcends it that man is able to face the absurdities of this world and still take it seriously enough to live responsibly within it. "The believer whose existence as eschatological is something *new* accepts responsibility for the world with a new urgency."[46] Obviously, Bultmann's view of eschatological existence has significant implications for the doctrine of man and his salvation, and for ethics, setting as it does the balance between indicative and imperative. This, too, will be traced in more detail in Part III.

e. Conclusions

We have been looking first in broad outline and then in more detail at Bultmann's view of the structure of history, particularly at the way he focuses attention on the dimension of personal history. Because for him *Geschichtlichkeit* is preeminent, Bultmann asserts that the ultimate reason for studying history is to become conscious of human existence.[47] Meaning in history is therefore to be found primarily in our own personal history.

Because of the wide acceptance of the slogan: "Christian faith is rooted and grounded in history," an understanding of history that elevates the personal dimension is bound to have significant implications for Biblical interpretation and theology. When the meaning of history is seen to reside primarily in "the history which everyone experiences for himself,"[48] the theological relevance of the history of Israel becomes an open question. The assertion that God reveals himself in "mighty acts" which constitute salvation history becomes doubtful or at least debatable. The Bible is now heard as God's word only when approached with the questions of human existence. Belief in God as creator reflects self-understanding rather than cosmological information. The history in which the cross creates a new situation is personal history. Forgiveness is the means by which new self-understanding becomes possible. These and other implications of this view of history will be the main topics for discussion in the rest of the book.

One final note before leaving Part I. Bultmann's stress on the primacy of personal history obviously invites the charge of subjectivism. But before we make a judgment on this, we ought to recognize that Bultmann himself sees the danger and hastens to affirm that in concentrating on *Geschichtlichkeit* he does not intend to deny the importance either of past historical events or of encounters in the present between the self and others. On the contrary, he insists that there is no historicity without such events and encounters. *Geschichtlichkeit* is constituted in decision, and decisions are not made in a vacuum. They are made only in the context of encounter with the neighbor and therefore in response to the claims of God.[49] Whether by arguing in this way Bultmann is able to refute the charge remains to be seen. In the meantime we should not prejudge the issue but leave the question open to be discussed later.

Part II

HISTORY AND THEOLOGICAL METHOD

3
THE PROBLEM OF HERMENEUTICS

BULTMANN'S WHOLE ENDEAVOR can be seen as an attempt to establish a coherent and consistent theological method of Biblical interpretation, one that makes use of historicocritical insights, at the same time recognizing the centrality of the kerygma and its validity for modern man. In the Epilogue to his *Theology of the New Testament,* Bultmann acknowledges the essential role of the historicocritical and *religionsgeschichtliche* schools, and indicates that as far as the use of the critical method is concerned, his own work stands in that tradition. But he goes on to insist that while it is essential, this approach is still only preliminary. It must "stand in the service"[1] of New Testament interpretation which begins only where criticism has ended.

What, then, is the method of interpretation that makes use of critical insights but goes beyond them? This, Bultmann says, is the basic question not only of New Testament interpretation as such but of theological method as a whole. In an early essay[2] in which he inquired into the relation between exegetical theology, systematic theology, and historical theology he insisted that only expediency should separate the work of the exegete and the dogmatic theologian. Their task is basically the same, namely, to explicate the existence of man in his relation to God by listening to the word of God that addresses him through the New Testament. Therefore, the question of how to use the results of Biblical criticism while at the same time interpreting the New Testament authentically so that it speaks to modern man in his existential situation is, for Bultmann, the question of theological method. This search for theological method leads Bultmann into three distinguishable but closely related areas.

The first is his concern with hermeneutics as he seeks to define the principles of interpretation of documents, the New Testament in particular. The second is the demythologizing project, in which he calls for an elucidation of these principles within a context of thought that is relevant to twentieth-century man. The third is the actual use of this approach and principles in the interpretation of the New Testament.[3]

a. The significance of the problem of hermeneutics

The importance of this problem has already been indicated in a preliminary way. For Bultmann, concern with hermeneutics is both deeper and wider than the question of how the New Testament is to be interpreted. Deeper because, as we have just seen, the question of New Testament interpretation is at the same time the question of theological method as a whole. Exegesis is not, in the final estimate, to be separated from dogmatics. Wider because, for Bultmann, hermeneutics is not just the science in which rules are developed for the interpretation of literary texts. Following Dilthey, he asserts that hermeneutics is "the science of understanding history in general."[4] This means that the Biblical writings as reflecting the historicity of man (in this case in his relation to God) must be subject to the same hermeneutical rules as those which apply to any other historical texts. Therefore, the question of Biblical hermeneutics is part of the larger question of hermeneutics in general.

Some of Bultmann's critics have recognized the central importance of the hermeneutical question.[5] Others have not, but the misunderstanding that results from this failure only serves to emphasize the importance of the question. Gustav Wingren, for instance, shows a lack of appreciation for the depth of the hermeneutical problem when he indicates that his method of evaluating the work of Nygren, Barth, and Bultmann will be to compare what these theologians say with "the conception which the Biblical writings themselves represent."[6] But how are the Biblical writings to be interpreted so that their representations are clear? Wingren does not raise this hermeneutical question, but he cannot avoid its implications. This becomes clear in his later discussion of Bultmann where he asserts that the only question he has asked is whether Bultmann's anthropological presuppositions are tenable on the basis of Scripture. But he should have asked: "Tenable on the basis of whose interpretation of Scripture?" for when he begins to criticize Bultmann (and Barth and Nygren too, for that matter) he actually uses not the weighty two-edged sword of "the Biblical writings themselves" but rather the lighter weapon of his own understanding of these writings. This is not to criticize Wingren for using the pen rather than the sword, but simply to point out that he is using an interpretative pen just as Bultmann is. So the question is whether Bultmann's pen is mightier than Wingren's, not whether it is mightier than the sword of the Bible.

Bultmann's reply to Walter Klaas[7] therefore applies with equal force to Wingren and to others who demand a hearing of Scripture without asking how it is to be interpreted:

> Walter Klaas upholds against me this proposition: "Whoever allows Scripture alone to be the criterion and yardstick of preaching, whoever holds the word of the prophets and apostles to be foreordained and repeats it, as he has responsibly heard it, is carrying out the interpretation of Scripture." Such words merely show that the man who pronounces them has still not got the perspective of the problem of the interpretation of the Scriptures at all. The exegete is to "interpret" Scripture after he has responsibly "heard" what Scripture has to say! And how is he to hear without *understanding*? The problem of interpretation is precisely that of understanding.[8]

Bultmann develops the same point more extensively in his article "Is Exegesis Without Presuppositions Possible?"[9]

b. *General hermeneutics*

In asserting that the problem of interpretation is that of understanding, Bultmann also acknowledges that there are a number of ways in which any writing may be understood, and that the way in which it will be interpreted will depend upon the preliminary understanding and the purpose for which the reading is being undertaken. But he also insists that while some texts can be interrogated mainly for information about past happenings and conditions, others such as works of art, history, and religion should be understood existentially. What does he mean by this?

First, he means that such understanding is not possible so long as one takes the point of view of a detached observer. Seeing the problem of understanding and recognition as Plato poses this in the *Meno*, Bultmann agrees with Dilthey that some preliminary relationship must exist between interpreter and text if what is apprehended is not to be completely alien and therefore incomprehensible. Therefore, at the most elementary level a prerequisite for understanding is met because "the expositor and the author live as men in the same historical world, in which 'human being' occurs as a 'being' in an environment, in understanding intercourse with objects and fellow-men."[10] But recognition of living in the same world, while a necessary criterion, is not a sufficient one for existential understanding.

Second, such understanding arises only when there is concern on the part of the interpreter for what the author is expressing in the text. The interpreter must be involved with and share the author's concern. In other words, while *no* understanding emerges from the reading of a text unless there is an active grappling with the writing by putting questions to it, there is no *existential* understanding unless these questions coincide with the author's. So, for instance, it is both possible and instructive to read the dialogues of Plato, putting the question of what life was like in Athens in those days. But the answers to that question give rise to existential understanding only if they stand in the service of further interpretation that concerns itself with the questions that Plato was wrestling with as he wrote.[11]

Third, Bultmann indicates that there is another prerequisite for existential understanding. He asserts that in fact the underlying concern expressed in works of poetry, history, philosophy, and religion is the problem of human existence. The basic questions are: What is man? Why is he here? How should he live?

And if the problem is approached as *my* problem, so that in asking the question of human existence I am putting my own existence at stake (Who am I? Why am I here? What should I do?), and if I am ready to respond to the possibilities of *self*-understanding with which such a text confronts me, then my relation to the text is that of existential understanding. Bultmann puts it this way:

> Real understanding does not arise from the satisfying contemplation of an alien individuality as such, but basically from the possibilities of human being which are revealed in it, which are also those of the person who understands, who makes himself conscious of them in the very act of comprehension. Real understanding would, therefore, be paying heed to the question posed in the work which is to be interpreted; to the claim which confronts one in the work; and the fulfilment of one's own individuality would consist in the richer and deeper opening up of one's own possibilities.[12]

Genuine understanding of a historical or religious text is therefore at the same time an act of self-understanding. And since Bultmann sees man in terms of historicity (*Geschichtlichkeit*) rather than as natural essence or rational entity, self-understanding cannot be achieved unless this affects man in the very core of his being. It is not possible for man to enter a situation of genuine decision and encounter and to leave it essentially the same subject. Therefore true understanding, which comes through decision and encounter only, is possible only within a relationship of involvement with the text in which one's own existence is constituted.

It is clear that for Bultmann, existential understanding depends upon asking the right questions (those the authors are concerned with) in the appropriate way. But there appears to be an obvious fallacy in this. How can we know ahead of time what questions to ask and how to ask them? Bultmann sees the problem and acknowledges that the method he advocates depends upon the possibility of a preunderstanding (*Vorverständnis*) of the text. This is not to be in any sense a detailed knowledge; how could it be? But neither is it simply a prior acquaintance with the general subject matter of the text. It is also an understanding of human existence that serves as a framework for questioning. Without such an understanding the questions that are essential to the whole enterprise would not even begin.

This may solve one difficulty, but others remain. The most obvious is that preunderstanding easily becomes prejudging. How can there be both preunderstanding and scholarly integrity? This question is best considered in specific rather than general terms, and will therefore be pressed in more detail in the next section when we consider how Bultmann proposes to apply existential hermeneutics to Biblical texts. However, it ought to be said at this stage that Bultmann acknowledges lack of objectivity in one sense of the word. Objectivity of the kind demanded in natural science is not appropriate when historical texts are being considered. As our discussion of Bultmann's *Natur-Geschichte* distinctions has already shown, he considered that facts of the past do not become part of history at all until they are of existential significance for a subject who stands within history and is involved with it.[13] In a sense, therefore, existential interpretation is subjective rather than objective. However, this does not necessarily imply arbitrariness. To be subjectively involved is not, for Bultmann, to manipulate the inquiry so that the desired conclusion is fabricated. Exegesis "without presupposing the results of the exegesis . . . is not only possible but demanded."[14] But to demand that the interpreter shall renounce his involvement and suppress his individuality is, as Bultmann says, absurd.

The distinction that Bultmann is drawing here between objective in the sense of "detached" and objective in the sense of "intellectually honest" is clear enough, and not likely to be challenged. What is not so clear is his contention that this involved yet honest approach is appropriate for the historian but not for the natural scientist. In fact, it seems absurd for Bultmann to press this distinction between methods of approach as far as he does. His distinction between *Natur* and *Geschichte* on grounds of content is useful, and it is true that man may be studied in such a way that he is seen as a natural phenomenon rather than a historical being. But it is not the natural scientist's detached approach that puts man in that category; it is simply the context in which man is being studied. It does not follow that because "man" is being studied in relation to his natural environment, and is therefore being seen as part of *Natur* according to Bultmann's schema, that the natural scientist is suppressing the kind of passionate concern for his subject matter that is demanded of the historian. If the historian can be involved without losing the discernment and integrity required of a scholar, then so also can the natural scientist.

c. Biblical hermeneutics

As we have seen, Bultmann holds that the Biblical writings are subject to the same principles of interpretation as other writings. This means, in general, that the Bible will remain silent until approached with questions, and that genuine understanding results only when these questions coincide with those the writers were concerned with. And it means, in particular, that the Bible as a historical document is genuinely understood only when approached with the question of existence, my existence, foremost in mind. The obvious concern for the *Geschichtlichkeit* of man that the Bible displays shows that it is a historical document, and therefore the right question to put is that of human existence. So Bultmann says:

> I approach the Biblical texts with this question for the same reason which supplies the deepest motive for all historical research and for all interpretation of historical documents. It is that by understanding history I can gain an understanding of the possibilities of human life and thereby of the possibilities of my own life.[15]

This *Fragestellung*, or "putting of the question," of human existence as primary in the approach to the Bible has influenced Bultmann's work in two significant ways which will be mentioned here and enlarged upon later. The first is that this concern for human existence provides the norm for Bultmann's interpretation of the New Testament, and leads him to use the theology of Paul and John as his key to all the rest (rather than, for example, Luke-Acts) because in them believing self-understanding in relation to the kerygma is clarified directly.[16] The second is that Bultmann reinterprets traditional theological formulations so that man and his existence become the major points of reference. So, for instance, he interprets the theology of Paul in terms of the antithesis "man prior to faith" and "man under faith," subsuming such topics as "the righteousness of God" under the heading "man under faith." This leads to the accusation that he replaces theology with anthropology, the force of which we shall consider in the next chapter.

Of course, in order to raise the appropriate questions it is necessary to have some preliminary knowledge of the context out of which the questions arise and to which the answers come. Therefore it is necessary not only to know ahead of time that the Bible is basically concerned with human existence but also to have some preunderstanding of existence so that the questions will be relevant and productive of meaningful answers. Agreeing with Barth that this preunderstanding is not to be seen as a positive natural revelation, Bultmann says that this is to be found within man's ceaseless questioning about himself. This is, if he only knew it, a quest for God:

> In human existence an existential knowledge of God is alive in the form of the enquiry about "happiness," "salvation," the meaning of the world and history; and in the enquiry into the real nature of each person's particular "being."[17]

But while everyone has these questions, they are usually nebulous, confused, and even contradictory. So Bultmann goes on to insist that before such questions about our own being can provide a useful preunderstanding, they should be at least examined and put in some order. This, he believes, has already been effectively done by Heidegger.

Bultmann's widely criticized use of Heidegger's categories or "existentials" is thus based on the conviction that inquiries into the "real nature of each person's particular being" can provide *existentiell* knowledge of God, and that Heidegger's particular inquiry effectively elucidates the question of existence as it arises within the human situation. But why Heidegger's elucidation? John Macquarrie has already dealt with this question and its various ramifications very thoroughly in his well-known comparison of Bultmann and Heidegger,[18] and there is little that can be usefully added to that discussion. However, for our purpose it is interesting to see how Bultmann's view of history has made Heidegger so acceptable to him. As we have already seen, Bultmann's approach to history implies a rejection of the traditional subject-object relation between a human being and historical events, and consequently of the view that to do history is to investigate past events. Therefore, in his approach to the New Testament, which poses the primary question of human existence, Bultmann is bound to reject the preunderstanding of existence and historical event that is provided by the classical subject-object ontologies. Only in this way is he able to sustain his insistence that what makes the Bible historical is its concern for *Geschichtlichkeit* rather than its concentration on past events. Gogarten has seen this clearly where he asserts:

> The crucial problem of history, if it is understood in this way, is the problem of hermeneutics, that is to say the problem of an interpretation which approaches history not from the outside but from within the historical character of human existence.[19]

It is just this approach to history from "within the historical character (*Geschichtlichkeit*) of human existence" that Bultmann sees in the work of Heidegger, thus providing him with an alternative to objectivizing ontologies that view man in natural rather than historical terms.

d. Philosophy or theology?

This hermeneutical procedure of coming to the text with the questions of human existence, and particularly of structuring these questions according to Heidegger's analysis of *Dasein*, obviously lays Bultmann open to the charge of forcing the Christian message into the distorting shape of the philosophy that provides the preunderstanding.[20] That it is not Bultmann's intention to impose alien philosophical categories on the Biblical witness is clear enough. His use of existentialism is part of a comprehensive solution to the whole problem of hermeneutics and therefore any criticism of his use of existentialist philosophy must recognize this as only one part of the larger endeavor which has at its heart, as Bultmann repeatedly asserts, the concern for hermeneutics. But although this is not Bultmann's intention, the question whether his solution nevertheless does lead the gospel into philosophical captivity must still be put. I conclude from my reading of Bultmann that whatever he actually does in interpretation, his hermeneutical procedure does not necessarily lead to the new kind of Babylonian captivity that Barth forecast, and I intend now to support this conclusion.

It is self-evident that interpretation always employs some categories or thought forms of the interpreter, whether he is aware of them or not. There is therefore no need to rehearse examples, as Bultmann does, in order to support his claim that "every interpreter brings with him certain conceptions, perhaps idealistic or psychological, as presuppositions of his exegesis."[21] But what are these conceptions or presuppositions to be? For Bultmann, those of Heidegger's existentialist analysis. Now, if some are necessary for any interpretation, the use of the ones Bultmann chooses is illegitimate only if (i) there is in fact another set of concepts which is intrinsically Christian and which should therefore be used instead; or if (ii) God speaks his word in such a way that the concepts necessary for the understanding of this word are created by the word itself; or if (iii) the existentialist philosophy which provides the preunderstanding actually substitutes its own content for that of the Christian message. These possibilities will now be examined.

(i) Some views of the inspiration of Scripture seem to imply that the set of concepts which is intrinsically Christian is the one actually found in the Bible and that no others can be vehicles for Christian understanding. I cannot accept this view, for while the framework of language and thought found in the New Testament is "Christian" in the sense of being that within which the kerygma was originally proclaimed, this does not warrant the conclusion that this is the only framework that is Christian, whatever status we give to language. For if we hold that only the Word of God is divine, then the words of the New Testament are human and therefore not uniquely qualified to express the divine Word. If, on the other hand, we claim that the human concepts which conveyed the divine were thereby transformed, then this power of transformation ought to be equally effective when other concepts are used. Bultmann's approach should not, therefore, be rejected on the grounds of using non-Christian thought forms.

(ii) Bultmann's use of existentialist categories would disqualify his method for those who take the Barthian view that God's Word creates the conditions for its own understanding at the same time that it breaks in upon man. It is interesting that Barth himself exonerates Bultmann from the charge of substituting philosophy for theology. Acknowledging that philosophical fragments float in the theological soup of all of us, Barth insists that Bultmann's claim that he makes only instrumental use of existentialist categories, and is therefore not dominated by them, should be accepted. He concludes that "in no case are we able to say that Bultmann is a philosopher and not a theologian."[22] But strange as it may seem, Barth has not stressed the real difference between his own view and that of Bultmann, which is that Barth's view of revelation would destroy the very basis for Bultmann's use of these existentialist categories. As we have already seen, it is because he thinks that there is already in every man an existential concern that is in fact a quest for God that Bultmann begins the search for an acceptable set of concepts (*Begrifflichkeit*) with which to structure this quest. In a passage that surely ought to elicit another Barthian "*Nein!*" Bultmann claims: "The question of his own real being which engages the attention of the man who seeks to be himself and has lost his self is the point of contact for God's word."[23] It is just because Heidegger elucidates this lostness and sharpens the point of contact that Bultmann makes use of his ideas. So if one rejects all such talk of the point of contact already existing in man, even when the *Anknüpfung* is understood negatively as man's need and not possession, then this should lead also to a rejection of Bultmann's main reason for using Heidegger. However, if one accepts, as I do, the legitimacy of speaking of man's need as the place where God's word is heard, then the use of Heidegger does not necessarily lead to a distortion of the kerygma.

(iii) But does the use of existentialist categories result in the replacement of Christian content by existentialist philosophy? Does an existentialist analysis of the way man questions his own being predetermine the kind of answer that will be found in the New Testament? Bultmann acknowledges the dilemma that faces every interpreter, which is that although he must use some philosophical concepts, there is no right philosophy "in the sense of an absolutely perfect system."[24] But he claims that today the philosophy that offers the most valuable perspective from which to view man is existentialism, particularly because it is the *least* likely of all to predetermine the answer by the form of the question. Existentialism is not concerned with the attempt to provide a pattern of human existence in the sense of giving a program of how man ought to exist. It simply clarifies the question of human existence by providing formal concepts. The point at issue here is clarified by an illustration which Schumann uses and to which Bultmann replies. Schumann claims that if one raises the question of love, then the preunderstanding which on Bultmann's terms makes the question of love meaningful already predetermines the content of the answer. So Schumann says: "Each man's understanding of what love means for him would depend upon his understanding of love in the abstract."[25] It is hard to imagine a comment more open to direct rebuttal. In fact, it looks like the remark of a secret sympathizer giving Bultmann the opening for a devastating reply. The whole point, of course, is that the preunderstanding which an existentialist analysis of love provides is not in any sense an "understanding of love in the abstract." On the contrary, it asserts that there is no such thing. It does not give content to the concept "love" at all, but simply insists that love, whatever it is, cannot be known outside the relationship of love. So Bultmann replies:

> Existentialist analysis describes particular phenomena of existence, for example, the phenomenon of love. It would be a misunderstanding to think that the existentialist analysis of love can lead me to understand how I must love here and now. The existentialist analysis can do nothing more than make it clear to me that I can understand love only by loving. No analysis can take the place of my duty to understand my love as an encounter in my own personal existence.[26]

The necessary preunderstanding provided by existentialist analysis is thus an elucidation of the awareness of human existence which all men have in some form or another, and does not provide a rigid framework that necessarily predetermines the content of the answer.

My conclusion, therefore, is that Bultmann's solution to the hermeneutical problem does not *in principle* lead to a distortion of the Christian message. This now leads to the question of what *in fact* occurs when Bultmann follows this method.

e. Exegetical procedure

It becomes clear from reading his *Theology of the New Testament* that Bultmann uses the theology of Paul and John as he interprets it to be normative for understanding the rest of the New Testament. This is confirmed in the Epilogue, where Bultmann asserts that the purpose of his undertaking, which is to make clear believing self-understanding in relation to the kerygma, is achieved directly in the analysis of the theology of Paul and John.[27] It is achieved only indirectly in the other sections where the presentation is critical and where deviation from the norm is characterized as decline. So, for instance, Colossians and Ephesians are commended because "fundamental motifs of

Paul's theology remain alive in them,"[28] while the Christianity of the pastorals is seen as a "somewhat faded Paulinism."[29]

Why does Bultmann look on Paul and John as normative? Because he finds in their approach that which coheres with his own hermeneutical principles outlined above, namely, the primary concern with the question of human existence and the view of history that sees the dimension of *Geschichtlichkeit* to be paramount. He discerns in them an approach that transfers theological interest away from the cosmic realm in the direction of the historicity of the individual. So he cites Rom., ch. 7, as an indication of Paul's directing attention away from world history to personal history, claiming that here Paul has presented the course of history from Adam by way of the law to Christ in the form of an autobiography.[30] It is for the same reason that Bultmann interprets the theology of Paul under the headings of "man prior to faith" and "man after faith," asserting that:

> Since God's relation to the world and man is not regarded by Paul as a cosmic process . . . , but is regarded as constituted by God's acting in history and by man's reacting to God's doing, therefore every assertion about God speaks of what He does with man and what He demands of him. . . . Therefore, Paul's theology can best be treated as his doctrine of man.[31]

In the same way, in his treatment of the fundamental motifs of John's theology Bultmann insists that the concern is with man rather than with cosmos,[32] and eschatology is historicized so that its relevance is seen in the present existence of man.[33]

It ought to be emphasized that Bultmann's norm is the theology of Paul and John *as he interprets this*. This is not to suggest that the norm ought to be what Paul and John actually say rather than the interpretation of what they say; I certainly agree with Bultmann that there can be no exegesis without presuppositions, since understanding demands interpretation. What I am saying is that in his application of the norm Bultmann excludes from further consideration some sections of the New Testament because they do not respond to the hermeneutical principles he applies. These include not only other parts of the New Testament that are not consistent with his interpretation of Paul and John but also parts of what he acknowledges to be Pauline and Johannine. So what results from choosing and applying the exegetical norm is partial exegesis. Three examples will illustrate this.

(i) In one of his many expositions of the meaning of the eschatological event, Bultmann makes a typical reference to Paul and John:

> It is the paradox of the Christian message that the eschatological event, according to Paul and John, is not to be understood as a dramatic cosmic catastrophe but as a happening within history.[34]

But he acknowledges elsewhere in the same work that this is not the only view of eschatological event that is apparent in Paul. There are signs that Paul does accept "the sense of apocalyptic eschatology with its expectation of a cosmic catastrophe."[35] But having acknowledged this, Bultmann gives no further consideration of this other view. This method of approach in which a variety of views are acknowledged but only one selected for attention, leaving the others virtually ignored, is seen even more clearly in the next example:

(ii) In considering Paul's view of the Spirit, Bultmann writes: "By the term 'Spirit' . . . [Paul] means the eschatological existence into which the believer is placed by having appropriated the salvation deed that occurred in Christ."[36] So Paul is to be interpreted as understanding the Spirit in terms of possibility for human historicity. But at the same time he acknowledges that Paul has other views of the Spirit in which he is seen as a miraculous divine power,[37] or, in quasi-materialistic terms, as a substance.[38] But after having mentioned these other trends in Paul, Bultmann gives them no further consideration, dismissing them as not "really determinative for Paul's concept of the Spirit."[39] This discussion of Paul's view of the Spirit which appears in the *Theology of the New Testament* was already anticipated in the essay on demythologizing. There, after indicating that Paul does see the Spirit as a "mysterious entity" and "supernatural material," he concludes that in the last resort Paul clearly means by "Spirit" the "possibility of a new life which is opened up by faith."[40] In *History and Eschatology*, Bultmann follows the same procedure, acknowledging that in Paul there is an element of apocalyptic and a looking forward to a world-historical future. But he avoids coming to grips with these by using the formula: "To be sure . . . but—"[41]

(iii) The same kind of exegetical result occurs when Bultmann uses Paul and John as his standard for understanding other parts of the New Testament. So, for instance, in his exegesis of Col. 1:20 and Eph. 1:10 Bultmann detects the presupposition that "prior to Christ the world had fallen into disorder and contention." This he sees as a falling away from the Johannine historicizing of cosmic dualism, and concludes that "here Biblical tradition has been forsaken."[42] It would be more accurate to say that "here Biblical tradition as defined by a particular interpretation of Paul and John has been forsaken."

What I have been arguing here is not that Bultmann reads into the text of the New Testament an interpretation of human existence that he had already formulated independently, nor that he imports a concern for human existence that is nowhere to be found in the New Testament, but that in his own hands his hermeneutical principles lead to partial exegesis. Selecting certain themes in Paul and John and making these the standard for the interpretation of the rest leads Bultmann to give exegetical attention to only part of the New Testament. This, I think, allows his hermeneutical method as a whole to be called into question, because if some parts of the New Testament prove to be impervious to a particular hermeneutical approach, this may be, as Bultmann contends, because those parts represent a forsaking of Biblical tradition. On the other hand, it may be because the hermeneutical approach is not adequate for the task or because it claims too much. It was once thought that all swans were white; in fact, this assertion was used in logic textbooks as an example of a universally true proposition. Then black birds in every other detail the same as swans were discovered in Australia. It was concluded not that these birds were "essentially unswanlike," nor that they represented an aberration whose existence could be acknowledged but then ignored, but that there was something wrong with the method of classification that could not adequately deal with them.

f. Summary and conclusion

Underlying Bultmann's hermeneutical method is his view of the priority of the dimension of *Geschichtlichkeit* in the structure of history. Therefore, for Bultmann, to approach a historical text with the question that the text is primarily concerned with means putting the question of human existence. The Bible is recognized as a historical text and therefore requires this approach because its primary concern is with the historicity of man. Putting the question this way to the Bible implies that the norm for Biblical interpretation will be "relevance to man's existential situation." In order to structure this questioning, Bultmann uses Heidegger's existential categories because these avoid an objectifying ontology and are based on a view of the centrality of man's historicity. This hermeneutical approach does not necessarily lead to distorted exegesis, but in Bultmann's hands it does lead to partial exegesis. This may be because Bultmann does not apply his own principles properly, or because his hermeneutical approach is itself at fault. There is, however, another alternative, and one that I am inclined to accept, viz., that no hermeneutical approach can be expected to allow all parts of the New Testament to speak in unison or with equal volume. A proper recognition of the diversity of the New Testament witness supports this conclusion, and makes unnecessary Bultmann's attempt to achieve harmony by silencing those voices which appear to him to be off-key.

4
THE DEMYTHOLOGIZING PROJECT

IT IS NOT MY INTENTION to undertake a full-scale evaluation of the demythologizing debate as it has grown through a multiplicity of essays, critiques, rejoinders, commentaries, and so-called "post-Bultmannian developments." Nor do I want simply to give a summary of the project as Bultmann outlined it over a quarter of a century ago and has been explaining it ever since. The first would be worth doing but demands a work in which this was the sole aim. The second has already been done, with varying success, by a number of scholars, usually as the prelude to a strenuous criticism. Here the project will be examined only from the perspective that has been used from the outset—Bultmann's view of history—in order to show how this view shapes the reason for and the method of demythologizing, provides the means of validating the project, and also locates it as an integral part of Bultmann's theological system.

a. Why demythologize?

Although the continuing debate is valuable because it directs attention to an important issue, it can be misleading if it focuses on this aspect of Bultmann's work and so isolates it from the rest. One answer to the question, Why the demythologizing project? is that it arises inevitably out of the approach that Bultmann had been following for years. Although Wingren overstates the case when he says that everything in the keynote essay was "old and familiar,"[1] it is true that it should not have come as a surprise to those already familiar with Bultmann's writings, for the lines of construction were already present in his earlier works. Of course, in some of these he speaks of myth and the need to eliminate it in the way that was common to his generation of scholars, but by the early twenties he had already paved the way for the different kind of demythologizing that he elaborated in the 1941 essay. In his *Jesus* in particular, published in 1926,[2] Bultmann showed his concern to interpret rather than to eliminate those teachings of Jesus which were set within a mythological framework, and he indicated that the purpose which was to inform the interpretation would be "to gain clear insight into the contingencies and necessity of [one's] own existence."[3] Already Bultmann's concern to reinterpret Jesus' message is closely linked to the view of history in which the element of personal history is dominant. The three characteristic features of the demythologizing project as Bultmann spelled them out in 1941 were already present in this earlier work, viz., a concern to interpret rather than to discard myth, the underlying purpose being to elucidate one's own existence within the framework of a view of history in which *Geschichtlichkeit* is central. Bultmann himself clearly locates the project within the intention of his work as a whole, insisting that its main purpose is interpretation and that it is therefore a method of hermeneutics.[4]

We have seen that the demythologizing project grew out of tendencies long resident in Bultmann's thought, but this still does not answer the question of why demythologizing is necessary.

(i) First, Bultmann claims, demythologizing is required so that the Christian message may be heard by modern man. Of course the gospel would be better understood if translated into modern language but that is not the main point. The New Testament message itself, its central affirmation of the Christ event as well as its peripheral elements, is couched in terms that make it quite unacceptable to modern man. The main difficulty is not that modern man finds the New Testament incomprehensible. On the contrary, he thinks that he understands it only too well, and is obliged to reject it because what he takes to be an integral part of the message is excluded by his present understanding of the world he lives in. This unacceptable framework of ideas Bultmann calls "mythological."

In the original essay Bultmann defined myth as that form of thought which represents the transcendent reality to which it refers in terms of this world, the divine in terms of human life.[5] However, this definition, largely a carry-over from the "history of religions" school, was not satisfactory because it led too easily to the conclusion (which Bultmann did not want to draw) that any statement about an act of God is mythological. Acknowledging this difficulty, Bultmann revised his use of the term to make it refer to any view or expression that is *de facto* excluded by modern man's mind as it is shaped by the concepts of natural science. Of the New Testament world view he says:

> This conception of the world we call mythological because it is different from the conception of the world which has been formed and developed by science since its inception in ancient Greece and which has been accepted by all modern men. In this modern conception of the world the cause-and-effect nexus is fundamental. Although modern physical theories take account of chance in the chain of cause and effect in subatomic phenomena, our daily living, purposes and actions are not affected. In any case, modern science does not believe that the course of nature can be interrupted or, so to speak, perforated by supernatural powers.[6]

It is clear that on this basis a great deal of the New Testament kerygma would be classified as mythological. Since man's mind is today conditioned by the views of science, history, and the self that preclude such mythology, demythologizing is necessary in order that the significance of the Christ event may again be appreciated.

So Bultmann's argument runs. But is he being too naïve and uncritical in his acceptance of the "scientific world view"? Does he really understand it, or is he allowing a superficial reading of the conclusions of natural science to launch him into just one more attempt to bring the gospel up to date? Karl Jaspers is inclined to write off the whole demythologizing project at just this point, claiming that:

> Where questions of faith are concerned, the impact of modern science is no more disintegrating than that of the universal rationalism of earlier times. Only a basic misunderstanding of modern science . . . leads to such a conclusion.[7]

Pressing the point even further, he continues:

> Down to the present time this [modern] science has been accessible to the masses only in the form of final results referring to the totality of things, a form that absolutizes and distorts the actual results of science, giving rise to spuriously scientific total views. These reflect modern scientific superstition rather than real knowledge or insight into the meaning, content and boundaries of science.[8]

But while it may be true that modern science does not necessarily have a disintegrating effect upon the Christian faith for one who has an adequate understanding of both, this is beside the point. Bultmann's contention is that in fact what a large number of people take to be the scientific world view does have a disintegrating effect on their faith. Jaspers has tacitly conceded this by acknowledging that what has been "accessible to the masses" is a view of the totality of things that rejects as unscientific what the Christian faith seems to demand assent to.

A parallel may be drawn here with the impact of the theory of evolution on the Christian faith earlier this century. The initial effects of this impact were destructive because what so many took to be an integral part of Christian faith in God as Creator was denied by evolutionary theory. An acceptance of Darwin's views entailed a rejection of the Genesis account of creation and fall as scientific fact. To have objected that Darwin's views were not identical with the popular understanding of them or that there were some flaws in his theory would have been beside the point. There was enough truth even in the popular version to make the literal understanding of the Genesis account no longer possible. What was needed was the recognition that Christian faith does not demand such understanding, thus leaving the way open to a new interpretation of the doctrine of creation. So in the present debate, modern man's thinking is in fact conditioned by an outlook (whether scientific, pseudoscientific, technical, popular, is beside the point) that makes it impossible to accept the idea of God as a being who makes spectacular excursions from a supernatural sphere into the cause-

and-effect nexus of the world. Consequently, if the faith is to be meaningful to modern man, either he must be persuaded to give up his scientifically conditioned way of thinking and to return to that of the first century, or Christian faith must be expressed in terms that are not mythological according to Bultmann's second definition of myth. The first alternative Bultmann rejects for two reasons, both of them sound. Man cannot "revive an obsolete view of the world by a mere fiat."[9] Nor does he need to try, because there is nothing intrinsically Christian about first-century thought forms. Therefore, Bultmann concludes, the second alternative must be chosen, and this is his first answer to the question of why demythologizing is necessary. The thinking of modern man is so shaped by, and his daily life is so dependent upon, a scientific world view that the first-century thought forms in which the gospel is couched and which conflict with this view need to be reinterpreted.

(ii) However, there is a second reason for demythologizing, which arises not from "modern man" but from the New Testament itself. Bultmann claims that the mythological expressions of the New Testament are not merely obsolete and therefore unacceptable to modern man, but are also misleading because they distort the Christian message and tend to inhibit genuine faith encounter with the kerygma.

This distortion is due to what Bultmann sees as the ironic self-frustration of mythological thought. Myths are intended to point beyond themselves and beyond this world to powers which transcend the merely human dimension and which give to man and the world their ground and limit. Their purpose is therefore to confront man with an understanding of existence in which he acknowledges a power that transcends his knowledge and control. But this purpose is frustrated because myth speaks of this power in human and this-worldly terms, attempting to convey what is basically in another dimension by using images that simply extend or paint in garish colors features of this dimension. So, for instance, myth pictures eschatological existence as everlasting life, thus stretching the present dimension quantitatively instead of pointing to a new quality of life. The power of God in Christ is mythologically presented as effecting this-worldly spectaculars rather than as a hidden dimension in the whole life of Jesus. The resurrection becomes a miraculous occurrence in world history rather than the lifegiving meaning of the cross. The Spirit becomes a quasi-material entity rather than a new mode of existence. This is what Bultmann meant by saying that "myths give worldly objectivity to that which is unworldly."[10] Once again it is clear that Bultmann's view of history is dictating the terms of the plea for demythologizing. Since, according to this view, man's faith relation to the event of salvation cannot be *historisch*—i.e., since the salvation event occurs in the present and therefore cannot be discerned as salvation event by *historisch* apprehension of a past occurrence—any expression that does represent the salvation event as happening objectively in world history is misleading and inhibits faith response. Such expression must therefore be demythologized so that faith may become a genuine possibility.

The view of faith that is operating here obviously owes much to Kierkegaard, who held that Christian faith is a total commitment of the self in the absence of all worldly security. Faith is in no sense a conviction that arises when historical research establishes the occurrence of an event in world history. Faith is the response of the self in the present to the word of preaching which does not locate an event in the past but constitutes it in the moment of encounter: "Faith . . . is both the demand of and the gift offered by preaching. . . . Faith is the abandonment of man's own security and the readiness to find security only in the unseen beyond, in God."[11] Unfortunately, myth inhibits this kind of faith response because it seeks to bring the act of God out of the unseen beyond and to locate it in *Weltgeschichte*. This leads to the view that the decision of faith is equivalent to an acknowledgment that a certain event took place in the past, and to an assent to certain propositions about that event.

It is precisely this view of faith as a kind of *historisch* decision about the past that Bultmann rejects. The Christian message, he insists, is not historical in the sense of giving an account of past occurrences that can be investigated and tested, confirmed or rejected, by historical research. It is historical in the sense of proclaiming the act of God that is decisive for man's historicity.

Therefore, it cannot be authenticated by any of the methods of the science of history. This is exactly the scandal that Bultmann insists must be preserved by demythologizing. Man demands verification for the assertion that, in preaching, the Word himself addresses man. He demands verification where, for genuine faith, there can be no such thing. So Bultmann is able to refute the common criticism[12] that he is merely trying to dilute the gospel so that the unbeliever may swallow it and "persevere in his faith with good conscience."[13] His intention is not to reduce the scandal of the gospel but to remove the false scandal of an outmoded world view so that the genuine scandal may make its impact, which is the proclamation that God acts in such a way that this may be received in faith but not verified prior to or apart from the event in which response is made. Therefore, demythologizing is necessary (and this is Bultmann's second answer) so that man can be confronted with the true decision of faith, a decision that has no objective basis for support and no ground for certainty outside the event of encounter and response.

b. How is demythologizing possible?

We have seen that for Bultmann the demythologizing project is made necessary both by the modern world view and by the nature of genuine faith. But how is such a project possible?

(i) It is possible in the first place because the world view within which the Christian message of salvation is proclaimed is not indispensable to the faith. Bultmann's own work in the history of religions and form criticism demonstrated that much of the New Testament is couched in Jewish apocalyptic and Gnostic thought forms. At times he is inclined to argue that when a concept is not unique to the New Testament, it ought for just this reason to be discarded as extraneous, or demythologized.[14] However, he generally argues more carefully that if there is a reason to demythologize, this should be done without compunction because the thought forms to be translated are not uniquely Christian.[15]

(ii) Demythologizing can be carried out, in the second place, because the myths themselves indicate their purpose, a purpose that is commendable but not successfully accomplished. This purpose, as we have seen, is to affirm that the life of the world and of man in the world is dependent upon God, who transcends the world and who gives the ground and limit of existence. Or, to put the same assertion in the context of the Christ event, the New Testament myths intend to affirm that God's act in Jesus Christ is like no other event in world history:

> It is precisely the mythological description of Jesus Christ in the New Testament which makes it clear that the figure and the work of Jesus Christ must be understood in a manner which is beyond the categories by which the objective historian understands world-history, if the figure and work of Jesus Christ are to be understood as the divine work of redemption.[16]

But, as we have seen, in attempting to show the non-*historisch* dimension of this event, myth attributed to the event special characteristics, and since these were still characteristics of a world-historical event it remained located as an episode in the past history of the world. The nonbeliever, looking at the "special characteristics" (the miraculous) rejects the event as impossible. The believer, accepting that the event occurred as described, is not called to any commitment apart from acknowledgment *that* this occurred. Therefore, neither believer nor nonbeliever is placed in a situation in which the response of faith is precipitated. However, because the *intention* of the myth is known, this can be retained if the transcendence of God can be proclaimed in such a way that faith is not replaced by assent, nor true scandal replaced by false.

(iii) Demythologizing can be carried out, in the third place, because Bultmann's view of history provides concepts that enable this intention of myth to be preserved while its objectivizing and faith-inhibiting features are removed. What is needed is a way of understanding the Christ event that enables us to say that it is both historical and eschatological, an event that is historical yet not confined to the past, an event that brings history to an end and yet takes account of continuing world history, an event that is discernible in history and yet not identifiable as anything decisive by any means other than acceptance in faith. Bultmann's understanding of history, including as it does the eschatological event that occurs in *Geschichtlichkeit* while having as its indispensable basis the *historisch* event of the crucifixion of Jesus, makes this possible. He is able to affirm that the event of salvation is an act of God that is historical because it occurs in personal history and eschatological because it occurs again and again, putting to an end one's past historicity and opening the way to the new. It is inextricably linked to the past historical event of Jesus of Nazareth, but the decisive nature of that event cannot be established by objective historical research. It is known only in the present faithful encounter with the message that proclaims it as decisive.

c. *Criteria and validation*

So far in this chapter we have been concerned with why demythologizing is necessary and how it could be possible, in each case seeing how Bultmann's view of history shapes his answers. But since Bultmann insists that demythologizing is simply a method of interpretation, we ought now to see how it measures up to his own hermeneutical principles which we discussed in the previous chapter.

(i) The first of these principles is that any method of interpretation is effective only if it brings questions to the text, and is valid only if these coincide with the questions the text is concerned to answer. Therefore, no interpretation of New Testament myths is valid if it bypasses the underlying intention of these myths. What is their intention? To point, as we have seen, to the power that transcends the world and human existence. This seems at once to invalidate Bultmann's demythologizing project, because he insists that the right question to put to the Bible is the question of human existence,[17] whereas if the myths are designed to point to the power that *transcends* human existence it would appear, at least prima facie, that their intention would be preserved by concentrating on the transcendent power rather than on human existence. This insistence of Bultmann on the priority of the question of human existence[18] has been repeatedly criticized not only because it apparently reveals an internal inconsistency but also because it appears to replace theology with anthropology. Because the issue has become so important it will be dealt with in a separate section at the end of this chapter; in the meantime the question of whether Bultmann has failed to preserve the intention of the New Testament myths by concentrating on human existence will be left in abeyance.

(ii) Bultmann's second principle of Biblical hermeneutics is that a valid interpretation of the New Testament must retain the intention of both the kerygma and the myth. The intention of the kerygma is to proclaim an event, an event that both elucidates human existence and also grants the possibility of new existence. It is on these grounds that Bultmann rejects the attempts of the older liberals, for not only did they try to eliminate rather than to interpret the myths but also, in reducing the kerygma to principles of religion and ethics, they returned to a nonhistorical view of Christianity whose essence was timeless truth rather than historical event. For them history held academic interest but no place of paramount importance in religion.[19] In the same way, Bultmann rejects the *religionsgeschichtliche* attempt, for here too the eventfulness of God's act is ignored. The Christian message is interpreted in terms of a mystical escape to a supramundane sphere, but this fails to recognize that the Christian's detachment from the world is an eschatological one that is granted him nowhere except in the event which at the same time makes him responsible for the world. Therefore:

> If the History of Religions school is right, the kerygma has once more ceased to be kerygma. Like the liberals, they are silent about a decisive act of God in Christ proclaimed as the event of redemption.[20]

So it is clear that for Bultmann no method of interpreting the New Testament is valid unless it retains the kerygmatic affirmation of God's decisive act in Christ.

Does Bultmann's own demythologizing approach stand up

any better to his criteria than the liberals and "history of religions" school? Our immediate answer is yes, because there is no doubt that his reinterpretation of the Christ event retains the insistence that in the eschatological event God himself is acting. However, this is only a provisional conclusion, because this insistence by Bultmann has been challenged from at least three directions. First, there are those who say that while he does speak of the act of God in the eschatological event, the historical nature of the event has been destroyed. Second, there are those who hold that while Bultmann continues to speak of an act of God in Christ this contravenes the terms of his own demythologizing. Those who make this criticism do so from two different sides: those who want to remove the contradiction in order to carry out demythologizing to its logical conclusion and those who want to remove the contradiction by retaining the event and rejecting demythologizing. Before these criticisms can be adequately dealt with, it is necessary to look more carefully at Bultmann's view of Christ as the eschatological event. This will be done in Chapter 6, when the above points will be taken up in detail. Now we can return to the question of whether Bultmann has substituted anthropology for theology.

d. Anthropology or theology?

One of the most common criticisms made of Bultmann is that the hermeneutical method which finds particular expression in his plea for demythologizing substitutes anthropology for theology.[21] By concentrating on the question of human existence, so it is said, Bultmann transposes the New Testament proclamation about God into assertions about man. And of course what is criticized is not simply the anthropological nature of the assertions but the method of interpretation that produced them. So Barth, in his essay on Bultmann, asks in typically rhetorical fashion:

> Can I understand and interpret my faith in any other way than in looking away from myself in the direction of Him who calls me in the message which I believe? Can the understanding of the New Testament be any other kind of "exis-

> tential" act than this: that I, in contradiction to all that I think and know of my existence, am forced to give up all understanding and all interpretation of myself . . . am caught up in looking toward Another?[22]

In answer to this line of criticism which insists that theology must be concerned with God rather than with human experience, two things must be said.

First, Bultmann is not attempting to substitute statements about man for statements about God. He is concerned to show the relation between the two because he is convinced that it is impossible to separate them. While statements about God and about man are not identical, they nevertheless necessarily imply one another. He is therefore ready to agree that theology is at the same time anthropology, and enlists the aid of Paul to support his view:

> Every assertion about God is simultaneously an assertion about man and vice versa. For this reason and in this sense Paul's theology is, at the same time, anthropology. But since God's relation to the world and man is not regarded by Paul as a cosmic process oscillating in eternally even rhythm, but is regarded as constituted by God's acting in history and by man's reaction to God's doing, therefore every assertion about God speaks of what He does with man and what He demands of him. And, the other way around, every assertion about man speaks of God's deed and demand—or about man as he is qualified by the divine deed and demand and by his attitude toward them.[23]

The reference here to the historicity of God's act and man's response reminds us that it is because of his view of history rather than any covert humanist tendencies that Bultmann stresses their reciprocal relation. History as distinct from nature cannot be objectively approached and discussed. It can be apprehended authentically only if one is prepared to find in this history what is of decisive significance for existence in the present. Therefore, insofar as God reveals himself in history rather than in nature he can be known only in the encounter in which our own existence is at stake, and can be spoken of only as he is significant for *Geschichtlichkeit*. He cannot be objectively identified, nor can his actions become the subject of a discussion in which no acknowledgment is made of the fact that the actions are constitutive of one's own being. Any such "theological" discussion is fruitless. In fact, says Bultmann, it is not only fruitless but sinful because this reenacts the sin of Adam, who asserted the right to discuss God's commands as though he were superior to them.[24]

The second comment on the charge of anthropologizing has already been anticipated. Bultmann claims not only that statements about God *imply* correlative statements about man but also that statements about God are *possible* only when they are at the same time statements about man. This is based more on Bultmann's view of God than on his understanding of history and of language. The Lutheran affirmation of the hiddenness of God remains a central theme in Bultmann's theology,[25] and he never wavers from the view that God is known not as he is in himself but only as he reveals himself to man.[26] Therefore, all statements about God, including those of the Bible which, after all, is a human witness, are statements about God as he is known to men. There should therefore be no stigma attached to the recognition that theological statements are all anthropological in this sense of conveying how God makes himself known and how this impinges on man's life. The question is whether God remains the real theme even when man speaks of him in the only way open to him, i.e., as reflected in human experience.

To put that question another way: While it may (and, I believe, must) be admitted that men can speak of God only as he is known to them, does this imply that human self-understanding must become the focus of attention? As we have just seen, Bultmann does not eliminate theology in favor of anthropology, but it could still be argued that he replaces theology with anthropology in the sense of giving priority to the latter. This is the point that Barth makes in the third volume of his *Dogmatik:*

> They [theological propositions] are doubtless all related to human existence. They make possible and give a foundation to the Christian understanding of them, and so they become —in an altered form—definitions of human existence. But

> they are not so originally. Originally they define the being and activity of God who is *different* from man and who *confronts* man . . . and so for that reason they are not reducible to propositions about the inner life of man.[27]

Thus Barth, while acknowledging that there is an anthropological implication to theological propositions, insists that all such propositions must begin from the recognition of God as one who confronts man as the Other. Therefore, any attempt to translate these into terms which refer to the "inner life of man" must be rejected. Bultmann's project is seen as just such an attempt to translate the gospel message into truths about man's inner life or self-consciousness, which is at best a return to the "truths of reason" of Lessing,[28] and at worst a reduction of the gospel to something trivial or nonsensical.[29] This way of interpreting the "self-understanding" of which Bultmann speaks leads to further charges that he has done away with the need for any event or confrontation that lies outside human consciouness.[30] What response can be made to this line of criticism?

(i) It is an error to interpret Bultmann's concept of "self-understanding" in terms of "self-consciousness" as, for instance, Thielicke does when he asserts that by "understanding of human life" Bultmann means a "timeless abstract truth." Having made that definite but quite erroneous identification, Thielicke then proceeds to demolish Bultmann along with Schleiermacher, asserting that their views amount to the same thing.[31] In his reply, Bultmann acknowledges that his own lack of clarity may have given rise to Thielicke's misunderstanding and then he proceeds to straighten the matter out by distinguishing between an existentialist approach to human existence and an existential one. The first is a type of philosophical elucidation of human being in general, and does issue in "timeless truths." The second is not a philosophical analysis at all but simply an approach of the self toward life that is involved rather than detached, so that an understanding of events becomes at the same time self-understanding. It is self-understanding that is existential in this second sense that Bultmann is talking about, self-understanding which is achieved not by a type of philosophical investigation but by an existential appropriation: "In my existential self-understanding I do not learn what existence means in the abstract, but I understand myself in my concrete here and now, in my concrete encounters."[32]

This misunderstanding may have been Bultmann's fault. On the other hand, it may well have been an *ad hominem* device of Thielicke, for it is puzzling, to say the least, that he equates Bultmann's view of self-understanding with timeless truth in the same article in which he acknowledges the primacy of the existential motif in Bultmann's theology. It is one thing to criticize Bultmann for using existential motifs. It is another to criticize him for a view of self-understanding that is clearly excluded by these motifs. But to criticize him for both at the same time is nonsensical. The fundamental characteristic of existential understanding is that it is not theoretical and does not issue in truths that are "timelessly valid." On the contrary, it is practical in the sense of being "rooted in man's way of being as practically concerned with the world,"[33] and becomes real only as it is made real by decision in one's own existence. Faith as a mode of self-understanding is not a *Weltanschauung,* and consequently propositions of faith are not timeless general truths.

(ii) Once it is recognized that when Bultmann interprets the gospel in terms of self-understanding he does so against a background of existential motifs, this answers the charge of another group of critics who accuse him of effecting a "ludicrous reduction" of the gospel. Since Bultmann takes from existentialism the view of understanding in which not just the mind or consciousness of man but his whole self is involved, then "self-understanding" is not merely one aspect of man's being but his whole way of being in the world. Man's self-understanding is the all-important component of who he is. Ian Henderson saw this point very clearly and very early in the debate, and his summing up of the argument is most convincing:

> The Christian may be inclined to ask if God's travail brought forth so negligible a result as a change in his own way of looking at himself. He may, as Thielicke does, complain that in Bultmann's interpretation of Christianity, nothing happens except consciousness. But if one can once share Heidegger's standpoint, criticism of that kind can immediately be

seen to be quite beside the mark. What Bultmann considers to be God's intervention in Christ is very far from being negligible, for in fact no change could be more important than a change in one's consciousness of oneself. It is my consciousness of myself that makes me what I am. It follows that a change in that consciousness is a real change in me.[34]

The case for the prosecution in the charge that Bultmann dissolves the gospel in the acid of self-understanding rests on two contentions: that his view of self-understanding reduces God's saving act to a change in human consciousness, and that the need for an act of God apart from human consciousness is thereby removed. I have been defending Bultmann against the first by showing that his existential view of self-understanding involves far more than his critics were willing to recognize, and that to describe this as "timeless truth" is to distort the evidence, and that for Bultmann there can be nothing greater done for man than to effect a change in his self-understanding. What now of the other point, that Bultmann fails to take account of the act of God, who is "*different* from man and *confronts* man"?[35]

(iii) Once again, a recognition of the existential context of Bultmann's view of self-understanding provides the answer. Existential self-understanding arises only in encounter with that which is other than the self. This is an implication of the phenomenological point stressed in existentialist philosophy concerning the intentional nature of consciousness, viz., that along with human consciousness goes, as an integral element, the recognition that this consciousness is *of* something or someone other than the self. So, in the case of self-understanding, the self is aware not only of its "subjective state" but of itself as existing only in relation to others. There is therefore no self-awareness without awareness of the other. We have already seen that Bultmann rejects the view of man as one who possesses a nature which is his essential self and which manifests itself in various situations. He holds instead to a view of man as *Geschichtlichkeit*—one who is constituted in these situations of meeting and decision. Therefore, self-understanding cannot be the result of any contemplation of the self which exists essentially apart from others.[36] Bultmann puts these two ideas, of the intentional nature of consciousness and of the self as constituted in relation to others, together, and indicates that man is genuinely himself as he responds authentically in encounter with what is other than himself:

> This is not the "inner life of man" at all, which can be brought under observation while setting aside what is different from it and what it encountered (whether environment, fellow-man or God) . . . for [existential understanding] seeks to contemplate and to understand the real existence (in history) of man, who exists only in a living connection with what is different from him—only in encounters.[37]

In elaborating this point, Bultmann makes it quite clear that for him Christian faith implies an encounter with God, and that this encounter takes place not in some mystical contemplation, nor within man's inner life, but within the eschatological event in which God acts and man responds, the event that occurs when the meaning of Jesus Christ is proclaimed and heard.

We can therefore conclude that to proclaim the gospel in terms of human self-understanding when this is done, as Bultmann advocates in the context of existential motifs, does not imply a reversion to the view of Christian faith as "timeless truth"; nor does it necessarily exclude references to an event in which man is confronted by God, who is different from himself. On the contrary, for Bultmann, reference to this event of God's acting, the eschatological event in Jesus Christ, is the focus of Christian faith. The relation between this event and the life of Jesus of Nazareth will be discussed in Chapter 6.

Part III

HISTORY AND DOCTRINE

5
THE REVELATION OF GOD IN HISTORY

THE EXISTENTIAL APPROACH that Bultmann has used in his understanding of the structure of history does more than suggest a means by which particular events may be appropriated. Its aim is a new understanding of history as such, and therefore a different idea about what it is that makes an event "historical." Consequently, this reinterpretation of the nature of history and of historical event will be of major theological significance because Christianity claims to be, above all else, a historical religion. This is generally taken to mean that it is based on identifiable events of the past, but if the term "historical" is interpreted differently, the very basis of Christianity will be understood in a different way. What happens when this different view of history is applied will be explored in relation to three fundamental Christian doctrines, namely, the revelation of God, the person and work of Christ, and the doctrine of man.

a. Heilsgeschichte *approach rejected*

We can take as the defining characteristic of the *Heilsgeschichte* approach the affirmation that God reveals himself in history, particularly in his mighty acts which constitute the history of the chosen people Israel. These revelatory acts are not isolated but are connected together in a history, a salvation history, and God's act in Christ is located in this history.[1] Meaning in history is therefore to be found by looking to God's activity in history, and theology becomes recital of the events in which God has made himself known. Christian theology is a recital of God's revelation in history which is seen as culminating in the event of Jesus Christ.

In his review of Cullmann's *Christ and Time*,[2] Bultmann claims that difficulties in this view become evident as soon as one asks how the term *Geschichte* in the compound *Heilsgeschichte* is being used. For Cullmann, it appears to have the same connotation as it does in *Weltgeschichte*, but this Bultmann cannot allow. Why not? For two reasons, as we shall see in a moment. Before we get to these, it is important for us to realize that Bultmann is not in a position to reject the *Heilsgeschichte* view by saying that it is "unbiblical," because he acknowledges that in the New Testament, particularly in Luke-Acts, a sustained attempt is made to interpret faith in this way. A *historisch* account of the life of Jesus and of the early Christian community is constructed and related to events in world history.[3] Nor can he deny that again and again in the New Testament the significance of Jesus Christ is proclaimed by setting him in the context of other acts of God in the history of Israel.[4] He must therefore concede that Cullmann and others have a clear precedent in the Bible for their views, and may claim with some justification that the *Heilsgeschichte* view of revelation is simply an extension of this approach already found in the New Testament. But this does not silence Bultmann. He is aware that this approach has precedent in the New Testament and is quite prepared to criticize it when it appears there too, because he sees it as a rejection of the kerygmatic intention. So, in an evaluation of the work of the author of Luke-Acts, he says:

> He has surrendered the original kerygmatic sense of the Jesus-tradition. . . . Whereas for the eschatological faith not only of the earliest Church but also of Paul the history of the world had reached its end, because in Christ the history of salvation had found its fulfilment and hence its end, according to the viewpoint of Acts the history of salvation now continues. While for Paul, Christ, being the "end of the Law," . . . , is also the end of history, in the thought of Acts he becomes the beginning of a new history of salvation, the history of Christianity. Later on he will be regarded by universalistic thinking as the middle-point and turning-point of history.[5]

It is clear from this that Bultmann recognizes the basis in the New Testament for the *Heilsgeschichte* view. It is equally clear that he rejects both the original approach and its twentieth-century version for surrendering the kerygmatic intention that is present particularly in Paul and John. Bultmann finds this approach unacceptable for two reasons, both of them dependent upon his view of history and its relation to the Christian faith.

(i) At the most elementary level, he objects to the *Heilsgeschichte* approach because it demands the impossible; it demands that the process of history should be looked at as a whole so that a pattern of meaning may emerge. But, Bultmann says, this is impossible because there is no way of gaining the supra-historical vantage point needed to discern the pattern. Nor can meaning be found by extrapolating some meaningful core, "a line which, though not shorter, is yet infinitely smaller" than general history.[6] It is just not possible to identify some events among others in world history as acts of God and then to join them together into a "holy history" because, according to Bultmann, meaning does not inhere in past occurrences approached in a *historisch* manner. The Bible therefore cannot be viewed simply as recital of the acts of God because "the word of proclamation is no mere report about historical (*historisch*) incidents."[7]

The *Heilsgeschichte* theologian would, of course, agree that the revelation of God cannot be read off past happenings by *historisch* observation. He insists that these are recognized as God's acts only by the "eyes of faith," or some other capacity or insight that is not natural to man. But while this may seem to approximate Bultmann's demand for a *geschichtlich* approach, even this more existential version of *Heilsgeschichte*[8] Bultmann cannot accept because he insists that it is just such a genuinely existential appropriation of events in the history of Israel that is no longer an open option for the Christian. The history of Israel cannot become his history.[9]

> The Christian message cannot and may not remind its believers of the fact that God has led their fathers out of Egypt. . . . The history of Israel is not our history, and so far as God has ruled with grace in that history, this grace is not

meant for us. This means that the history of revelation is not the history of revelation for us.[10]

Why not? This brings us to Bultmann's second reason for rejecting the *Heilsgeschichte* view.

(ii) Bultmann's understanding of Jesus Christ as the eschatological event conflicts with the role that *Heilsgeschichte* assigns him. In Bultmann's view, he cannot be seen as the culmination of a series of events that occurred in the history of Israel and were witnessed to in the Old Testament, for, as we have seen, Bultmann holds that the significance of the term "eschatological" is not its reference to either past or future in world history but its transcending of this dimension. To speak of Christ as the eschatological event is to say something primarily about personal history. It is to affirm that he brings to an end man's past understanding of himself and grants the possibility of new existence. It is not to say that he is the *telos* of the historical development of a people, nor that he is the *archē* of another such history, the history of Christianity analogous to the history of Israel. He is the eschatological event in the sense of putting to an end the history of a particular people as the sphere of God's activity. To say that Christ is the end of salvation history is not to say that he is the goal of historical development, but that he puts to an end altogether this way of looking for the revelation of God.[11] This revelation is still in history, but in personal history, not in the history of a particular people. The history that is decisive is not world history, not the history of Israel or of any other people, but "the history which everyone experiences for himself."[12]

It is quite obvious that Bultmann's rejection of *Heilsgeschichte* views of revelation, whether contemporary forms or the New Testament prototype of Luke-Acts, is based on his view of history, particularly upon his interpretation of eschatological event. This leads him to assert that the only sense in which the history of Israel can be considered salvation history for the Christian is a negative one, the "history of miscarriage," and even this is possible only by looking in retrospect from Christ as the eschatological event who does not complete, but rather puts to an end, this history. The familiar diagram, so often seen on the blackboards of theological classrooms, of a time line of history leading smoothly up to Christ as the climax[13] (with perhaps a crest to represent the Sinai event and a trough the captivity) has now been erased. Still Bultmann maintains that God reveals himself in history. How can he continue to make this claim?

b. Bultmann's alternative

The term "salvation history" can mean either "history of saving events" or "history which saves." In the first case, the events themselves are looked upon as redemptive, and the history is the narration of these events. In the second case, it is not the isolated events that are seen as redemptive but the whole life of the people; history is not then narration but the redemptive process itself. Bultmann proposes an alternative to each of these ways of looking at salvation history.

In the first place, neither the history of the world nor the history of the empirical people Israel can be read as a connected account of God's saving acts. Such histories, Bultmann insists, are profane.[14] This is not to say that they are evil or Godforsaken, but that they are "secular" according to the currently popular way of using that word in theological discourse. In other words, world history should not be read either in its entirety or in isolated incidents as the arena in which God's revelation becomes visible. We should not expect to find some clue that enables us to view the whole of history, as Hegel did, as the unfolding of the Absolute in time. Nor should we try to select certain events, for instance in the history of Israel, in the hope that by connecting them together God's revelation will emerge, as the hidden picture does in a child's dot-to-dot puzzle. As far as Bultmann is concerned, the current secular theologies that urge us to look for God's action in the world rather than in the church are not secular enough. They do not take seriously enough the radical secularity of world history. It is easy to point to the inherent difficulty of these theologies which call Christians to join God "where the action is—in the world," for how are we to discern just where God *is* at work? How do we distinguish his spirit from the other spirits, his power from the powers, his authority from the authorities? A number of men have wrestled with this problem, among them Colin Williams and Gregor Smith, and it was also faced at the recent Assembly of the World Council of Churches at Uppsala, and none have attempted to avoid the difficulty. However, for Bultmann this is more than a difficulty of establishing criteria. It is not just difficult, according to him, to establish criteria for recognizing God's activity in the world in this way; it is impossible. All such attempts are futile because they ignore the profane nature or radical secularity of world history. There is simply no way of distinguishing between events in the world and saying that this one is and this one is not an act of God. Instead, Bultmann insists, we should look into our own personal history, for if there is any such thing as a "history of saving events," it can only be a narration of God's saving activity within our own histories. This approach Bultmann finds already in the thought of Paul:

> While the history of the nation and the world loses interest [for Paul], another phenomenon is detected, the true historical life (*Geschichtlichkeit*) of the human being. The decisive history is not the history of the world, of the people Israel and of other peoples, but the history which everyone experiences himself. For this history the encounter with Christ is the decisive event.[15]

This does not solve all the problems of criteria and recognition, of course. Identifying the activity of God among all the forces at work in our personal histories is still a major difficulty. However, the point has been made that for Bultmann "salvation history" as history of saving events makes sense only as the account of God's saving work within one's own history.

In the second place, Bultmann recognizes that "salvation history" sometimes refers to a "history which saves." According to this view, God's revelation and saving activity are evident within the whole life of a people. To be saved then includes being grafted into this community and accepting the saving acts of God in that history as his saving acts for oneself:

> In the Old Testament, God's revelation is bound to a particular people's history. . . . Whatever God has done in this history He has done in each individual who belongs to the people and its history. Whatever God did when He raised up Moses, led the people out of Egypt, guided it through the desert and brought it to the holy land, He has done to each individual and does even now, since this history is not past, but is still present in every part of the people.[16]

It is clear from this that Bultmann's rejection of *Heilsgeschichte* is not based on any superficial misunderstanding of what is involved. He does not sell this view short, for instance, by misinterpreting the status of the events or the way they are appropriated, for he readily acknowledges that those who stand in this tradition confront the events of salvation as *geschichtlich* and not *historisch* events. His objection is that this is just not a live option for the Christian. Part of what it means to be a Christian is the acceptance of Christ as the eschatological event, and this means the end of the history of Israel as a saving history that can be appropriated as one's own. God's act, which is at the same time revealing and saving, is now known to man not as he appropriates the history of a people as his history but as he encounters in the present the eschatological event.

But how is this event to be made present? Not by making the history of a people my history, but by being confronted in the present with the kerygma. The eschatological is present, and becomes present again and again, in the proclamation of the kerygma, and can therefore become the decisive event that constitutes my personal history. To recognize the act of God in this event is at the same time to respond to, and receive, the grace of God which comes through the event. Revelation and salvation are therefore both aspects of the same event, and just as there is no salvation apart from our faithful participation in the event, so there can be no revelation of God apart from the event in which our own being is put in jeopardy by the word that is spoken and received:

> The act of God in Jesus Christ is not understood in the New Testament as analogous to a decisive historical event in the

> history of Israel by which through historical (*geschichtlichen*) connection, every later generation inherits what Jesus meant to his own. . . . The message of the forgiving grace of God in Jesus Christ is no historical account of a past event, but rather the word which the Church proclaims, which now addresses everyone directly as the word of God, and in which Jesus Christ is present as the "word."[17]

Once again, Bultmann's argument is likely to be convincing only to those who accept his understanding of history, and, in particular, his view of Jesus Christ as eschatological event within that schema. In the present discussion of revelation, this understanding has operated in two ways. It has so defined the eschatological act of God that this can no longer be seen within the context of world history, and has also provided the norm for accepting or rejecting New Testament passages offered as evidence for or against this definition. Thus if a New Testament passage is cited in which the revelation of God in Christ *is* still seen in terms of world history, such a passage can then be classified as inconsistent with the proper understanding of Christ as eschatological event. This is the procedure that Bultmann employs in his critical treatment of Luke-Acts, as we have seen.

The danger in this kind of argument is obvious. One can easily agree that there is a conflict between some parts of the New Testament and Bultmann's view of eschatological event, but then choose to reject not these passages but Bultmann's criterion, viz., his view of eschatological event. The point is that in some parts of the New Testament Jesus Christ *is* understood as "analogous to a decisive historical event in the history of Israel," and the parallel between participation in the life of Israel and in the life of Christ is frequently drawn. And Bultmann's claim that "the message of the forgiving grace of God in Jesus Christ is no historical account of a past event but rather the word which the Church proclaims, which now addresses everyone as the word of God, and in which Jesus Christ is present" simply cannot be supported. In the Gospels, including the Fourth, a historical account of a past event is precisely the form that the church's word takes.

Why does Bultmann make such a generalization, one that can be supported only by the exclusion of so much New Testament material? Because, in his view, these sections cannot be the vehicle for genuine revelation. For him, revelation occurs only in existential event; not when the past is recited, but when present existence is challenged; not when a man finds himself part of the life of a people, but only when he is confronted by the decision that constitutes his own life. But does Bultmann need to make these "not when . . . but" distinctions? I don't think so. Present existence may be effectively challenged when the past is recited; Bultmann's recognition of the kerygmatic rather than the *historisch* nature of the Gospels should have enabled him to see that. It was research of the kind that he initiated that has led to the present realization that the Synoptic (as well as the Fourth) Gospels were concerned not just to give a past historical narrative, but to proclaim the meaning of the Christ event in order to elicit response. By the same token, finding oneself part of the life of a people by no means excludes decision within that historical context which is at the same time constitutive of one's own *Geschichtlichkeit*. Only a very myopic view of the Old Testament could ignore the prophetic call for continuing individual appropriation of the faith of the community and the call to individual decision based on the expectation of a new covenant and a new identity as a people.

Therefore, to understand God's act in Christ in terms analogous to a decisive event in the history of Israel which individuals may appropriate through *geschichtlich* encounter is by no means incompatible with Bultmann's view of revelation as event which occurs only when existential response is elicited. If Bultmann had seen that, it might have prevented him from using his view of eschatological event as an arbitrary hermeneutical device which simply excludes from consideration significant parts of the New Testament that appear to conflict with it.

c. *Revelation and the Old Testament*

Bultmann insists that seeing Christ as eschatological event means the end of viewing the history of the world or of nations as the sphere of revelation. God is now seen as revealing himself in personal history. But since the Old Testament clearly affirms that God *does* act in the history of nations, Bultmann now faces the problem of how the Old Testament can be taken seriously by Christians at all.

It might appear at first sight that Bultmann invokes the Marcionite solution. In an article on the significance of the Old Testament for Christian faith, he wrote:

> For the Christian faith, the Old Testament is no longer revelation as it had been, and still is, for the Jews. For everyone who stands in the Church, the history is no longer a live issue . . . the history of Israel is not the history of revelation for us.[18]

But in case we are tempted to stop there, concluding that Bultmann is advocating the rejection of the Old Testament, or its retention on merely antiquarian grounds, we should read another excerpt from the same article:

> For anyone who has done even a minimum of historical reflection, it is senseless to try to hold on to Christianity and at the same time to discard the Old Testament. One should realize then that the Christianity he hopes to preserve is no longer Christianity. Either-or; both, or none at all.[19]

We have here the elements of an interesting puzzle. Bultmann does not accept the *Heilsgeschichte* view of God's revelation, and therefore does not see the Old Testament as recital of God's mighty acts, important for the Christian as prelude to the culminating act in Christ. Nor does he see the Old Testament as the embodiment of a tradition that can be appropriated as part of the Christian's own history. Yet he insists that one cannot hold on to Christianity if the Old Testament is discarded. But on what grounds is it to be retained?

Not, Bultmann insists, by a reversion to the *religionsgeschichtliche Schule* approach which demanded that both Old and New Testaments be viewed primarily as documents in the history of religion, and then examined to determine the type and stage of the religious development of the men who had produced these samples of sacred literature. Such an examination also implies that the religion reflected in the New Testament is a development out of that which produced the Old. Then the value of the Old Testament for the Christian (apart from its antiquarian interest for any anthropologist or historian, Christian or not) is that it reflects the beliefs of men at a certain stage of religious development, a further stage of which is the religion that gave rise to the New Testament writings.

This view of the value of the Old Testament is rejected by Bultmann but not for the reason usually advanced, viz., that this approach sees the Old Testament only in terms of man's ideas rather than of God's acts. His rejection is based on his *historisch-geschichtlich* distinction. The "history of religions" approach is a *historisch* one, being detached and objective, concerned only to bring to light facts about the past. It is not existential, and therefore does not convey the significance of the past for present existence:

> By considering both the Old Testament and the New Testament religions as past-historical (*historisch*) phenomena, its approach is from the outside and decides their relationship from an external and exalted position. It does not ask from the standpoint of the believer: What does the Old Testament mean to me, to the Church?[20]

Since he has ruled out both the *Heilsgeschichte* and *religionsgeschichtlich* approaches, it is not surprising that Bultmann maintains that the significance of the Old Testament for the Christian can be retained "only by understanding Old Testament history as history of salvation in a new sense."[21] But what is this new sense? In his writings Bultmann gives alternative views. The Old Testament may still be seen primarily as the history of Israel's relation to God, in which case it is salvation history for the Christian only in the negative sense as a history of miscarriage.[22] Or it may be viewed as a particular interpretation of man's existence, and in this case the Old Testament-New Testament link is less paradoxical, since the understanding of human existence is basically the same in each.[23] It will be worthwhile to look at these alternatives in more detail.

(i) Bultmann asserts that if Old Testament history is to be read by the Christian as the history of salvation, this is possible only in a paradoxical sense, for two main reasons. First, Old Testament history as the way of the law is a history of the "false way of salvation which led man into the miscarriage of his endeavours."[24] This way is perverse not so much because man finds it impossible to live up to the requirements but because it points man in the wrong direction, encouraging him to think that he may achieve his own righteousness.[25] It is in this sense that Old Testament history is the false way of salvation, or, in other words, salvation history only in a negative sense. Christ has put an end to this history. Now this history is no longer our history and must not become our history again.

Second, the history of Israel as salvation history is misdirected, according to Bultmann, in another sense. Not only its hope for man's righteousness under the law but also its hope for national fulfillment was misconceived. The meaning and the unity of salvation history were contained within the hopes of Israel as a nation, and again this can be viewed as salvation history by the Christian only in the negative sense of demonstrating that it is impossible to identify God's activity within the world with the history of an empirical people. Then the Old Testament witnesses to the miscarriage of nationalistic hopes, and Jesus Christ fulfills Old Testament history in the negative sense of showing this hope to be utterly ill-founded.[26]

(ii) If the Old Testament is approached not with the question, What does this say about the history of Israel? (which was the operative one in the previous section) but with the question, What does this mean to my present existence? a new possibility emerges for Christian understanding of the Old Testament. Bultmann follows this lead, which is obviously consistent with his own hermeneutical approach, by indicating that the Old Testament is significant primarily because it is law. It proclaims the law without which the gospel is meaningless to man. Following both Paul and Luther, Bultmann affirms:

> The existence under the Law, under the demand, is herewith understood as the prerequisite for existence under grace. . . . The Old Testament is thus the prerequisite of the New, not in the historical (*historisch*) sense that the historical (*historisch*) phenomena of the Christian religion have become

> possible only on the grounds of the historical-religious development declared in the Old Testament, but rather in the sense that man has in fact to stand under the Old Testament in order to understand the New.[27]

Again, the Old Testament is significant only in the negative sense of providing a contrast against which the genuine revelation is seen more clearly. But even this limited purpose could be achieved by other means. Any other literature that stresses the moral law under which all men stand would serve just as well as preparation for the New Testament message of liberation.[28] Therefore, the Old Testament as the embodiment of *specific laws* is no longer revelation for us, because these laws were applicable to a people and in an era different from ours. Nor is it uniquely revelation in the sense of providing the demand of law *in general*, for any other body of law that is similarly felt as demand would serve equally as well.

However, Bultmann insists, there is unique and irreplaceable value in the Old Testament for Christians, and it lies in its recognition of the *basis* of the law and thus of the origin of the demand that is laid upon us. This becomes evident when the Old Testament is approached with the question, How is the existence of such law and demand significant for me? The Old Testament answers this question in terms of the God-man relation, whereas other literature, while recognizing the demand under which we all stand, interprets this as the requirement of man's inherent dignity as man or as the ideal which has yet to be achieved. In other words, the Old Testament is unique because, in evoking the realization of the demand, it points to its origin in God the creator and our creaturely status. Therefore, the Old Testament becomes revelation for us as it sheds light on our existence as creatures of God. At the same time, the link with the New Testament is forged because in both Old and New the interpretation of man's creaturely existence is basically the same:

> Whoever reads the Old Testament is confronted with the question of whether he has to understand the knowledge of the "thou shalt" as referring to his dignity or to his creatureliness; whether he is to understand the demand under which

> he stands as the authorized system of justice by means of which he can achieve his dignity and the perfection of his personality, or as the demand which places him in obedience to God and in service toward his neighbour and which reminds him constantly of his imperfection and sin. The way in which the Old Testament understands man finds expression primarily in the belief in creation . . . this understanding of existence is the same as that of the New Testament, the same as the Christian as over against the Greek or humanistic or idealist views.[29]

So in the final estimate, Bultmann finds the significance of the Old Testament for the Christian to be in the understanding of human existence which is to be found there, and which in general corresponds to the Christian understanding.

There are three comments that I have about this approach of Bultmann to the Old Testament. First, he has given an effective warning against interpreting God's act in Jesus Christ as fulfilling Old Testament history simply in the sense of being the culmination of a series of past events of revelatory significance.

Second, he has established the importance but not, I think, the necessity of the Old Testament for Christian faith. The importance he has established on grounds consistent with his own views of faith and history, viz., that the proper approach is *geschichtlich* rather than *historisch,* and that the theologically relevant dimension of history is personal rather than national or world history. But has he succeeded in establishing its necessity on these grounds? The only reason Bultmann has given in support of his statement that it is "senseless to discard the Old Testament" is that in fact the interpretation of human existence found there coincides with that of the New Testament. Admittedly, he has shown very clearly how the Old Testament view of the basis of the law's demand differs from other views, but he has not demonstrated that any such prelude to the New Testament proclamation of grace is essential. If the same understanding of human existence as creaturely, as standing under the demand of God, is found in the New Testament, why, on Bultmann's terms, is the Old necessary? Why cannot Christianity be preserved without the Old Testament? It might, of course, be argued that the New Testament understanding of human existence arose out of the Old, so that the latter is "historically" necessary in a sense; but Bultmann has rejected (and, to be consistent, must reject) this along with all other attempts to establish a merely *historisch* connection between the two Testaments.[30]

Third, Bultmann is justified in seeing the significance of the Old Testament as he does as long as his hermeneutical principle —that of approaching the Bible with the question of human existence as primary—is accepted. Certainly, in both Testaments there is concern shown to answer this question. But this is not the only concern, nor was this the principle generally used in the early church to interpret the Old Testament. As Bultmann himself acknowledges, the principle of prophecy and fulfillment was the one normally used by the New Testament writers, although he is not prepared to follow their lead. Nevertheless, his understanding of the Old Testament is consistent with his own hermeneutical principles, and he has, by using these, established the significance of the Old Testament for the Christian on grounds other than those advanced by the "history of religions" or "salvation history" schools.

However, there is one other condition for Old Testament interpretation that Bultmann lays down, but this he himself fails to meet. He says:

> If the Old Testament is to be received into the message of the Church as God's Word, the inflexible condition [is] that the Old Testament be used in its original sense, although without its relation to the people of Israel and their history.[31]

Undoubtedly, Bultmann's method of approach does not depend upon retaining the relation between the Old Testament and the people Israel and their history; in fact, it depends upon breaking loose from the confines of that relation. But whatever other advantages this may have, it cannot claim at the same time to be using the Old Testament in its original sense. For if "original sense" refers to the intention of the Old Testament witness itself, then it is clearly impossible to eliminate its relation to the people Israel and their history; or if by "original sense" is meant the interpretation favored by New Testament writers and the early church, then the relation to the people Israel and its history was a dominant theme in that interpretation also.

I think that Bultmann has made an important contribution to the whole discussion of how a Christian should understand the Old Testament, and has done so in a way that is consistent with his hermeneutical principles, although he has not established that the Old Testament is essential to Christian faith. My main criticism is that he is too eager to break the Old Testament loose from its relation to the history of Israel. He does so because he thinks that the Old Testament understanding of the nation reflects only false nationalistic hopes that were put to an end in the eschatological event; he fails to acknowledge that already in the Old Testament there is found the pronouncement of God's judgment on such false hopes, and this was fulfilled directly and not paradoxically in Christ.

d. The "absoluteness" of revelation

We have seen that for Bultmann the history in which God reveals himself is personal history. This raises serious difficulties, for how can the excesses of subjectivism which thinks of God's revelation coming directly and privately be avoided? This opens the way to religious fanaticism—to the view that since God reveals himself directly, only the recipient really knows what God says. The believer is then secure from any external questioning or evaluation because it is in his history and only his that God's revelation can be known.

Of course Bultmann denies this implication. In his reply to Karl Jaspers, for instance, he insists that by "revelation in personal history" he does not mean "sudden illuminations within the history of the spirit."[32] But at the same time he denies any interpretation of this revelation which leads to objectification, any "fixation of God as an objective entity," any "misconceiving the revelation as an act accomplished once and for all."[33] The terms in the problem that Bultmann has to solve are now becoming clearer. As a Christian theologian, he insists on the absoluteness of the Christian revelation,[34] yet he rejects the view that God's revelation is an objective entity in the world, an act accomplished once and for all. He insists that God reveals himself in personal history, yet denies that this opens the way to a riot of unverifiable private interpretations of this revelation. He must therefore find a way of establishing the absoluteness of the Christian revelation on grounds other than the once-for-allness of an objectifiable event in the past, while at the same time avoiding "private illuminationism."

Bultmann begins by making the point that there can be no universally valid criterion by which God's revelation can be identified as such. If there were, this would elevate man above his status as creature wholly dependent upon the Creator. Man would then be judging God rather than being judged by God's acts, "as though God had to justify Himself to man."[35] Therefore, the revelation of God cannot be absolute in the sense of eliciting immediate recognition from the observer. That God is acting at all in the events that reveal him can be discerned only by the eyes of faith.

But what are these events which reveal God? For Bultmann, those which occur within personal history when one is encountered by the word that proclaims Jesus as the Christ. Therefore, revelation is not communication of teachings, and so its absoluteness cannot lie in the absolute or timeless quality of these teachings, whether ethical, philosophical, or historical. Revelation occurs within the event of encounter with the Word, an existential encounter in which there is no genuine hearing and understanding of God unless this precipitates self-understanding. As we have already seen, self-understanding is not speculative or timeless; it is constituted in the moment of existential decision. Therefore, Bultmann claims, the revelation of God in Christ is absolute because of the absolute nature of the decision with which this revelation confronts man. In this event, man is faced with the absolute distinction between two divergent modes of self-understanding as possibilities for existence. He is faced with the choice of living by God's grace or by his own works:

> When the revelation is truly understood as God's revelation, it is no longer a communication of teachings, nor of ethical

> or historical and philosophical truths, but God speaking directly to me, assigning me each time to the place that is allotted me before God, i.e., summoning me in my humanity, which is null without God, and which is open to God only in the recognition of its nullity. Hence there can be only one "criterion" for the truth of revelation, namely this, that the word which claims to be the revelation must place each man before a decision—the decision as to how he wants to understand himself; as one who wins his life and authenticity by his own resources, reason and actions, or by the grace of God.[36]

From this it follows that the event of revelation must always be in the present, for self-understanding is not an achievement which from then on makes a man secure in the knowledge of God and himself. It is an attitude of faith that needs to be renewed constantly in each situation in which man finds himself.

We can now see how Bultmann makes it possible to view the revelation of God as absolute without confining this to an objectifiable event of past history. It is absolute because it occurs again and again in man's present existence, demanding a decision of absolute or ultimate significance between two ways of self-understanding. But this still leaves one aspect of the problem unsolved, for this way of understanding "absoluteness" still has provided no safeguard against the threat of a plethora of private revelations.

At this point it becomes evident how important Bultmann's stress on God's revelation *in Christ* is. He insists that the event in *Geschichtlichkeit* which is at the same time God's self-disclosure and man's self-understanding occurs only through the proclamation of the Christ event. God's revelation does not occur when man contemplates nature or the mysteries of life or the depths of his own being, nor when he studies the history of nations and cultures, nor when he reads the lives of Socrates, Buddha, or Gandhi. The saving Word of revelation is heard only in the proclamation of Christ; only after this Word is heard is it possible to recognize in nature and in history the hand of the Creator:

> This finally is the significance, therefore, of the revelation in nature and history; it constantly refers us to the revelation of the forgiving grace of God in Christ. But it is only in doing this that it is revelation for us; and that means that, apart from Christ, it is not revelation for us.[37]

There is, after all, some test of authenticity that can be applied amid the clamor of individual voices claiming to know God's revelation. It is the question: Do these arise in response to the Word that proclaims Jesus as the Christ?

It may appear that we have now come full circle by reintroducing the once-for-allness of a past event in order to establish absoluteness without subjectivism. But in stressing the unique role of Jesus Christ in revelation Bultmann claims that he is emphasizing not its location in the past but its continuing impact when proclaimed in the present. The distinctive feature of what was a definite occurrence in the past—the life of Jesus of Nazareth—was not that it occurred then but that now it becomes the event through which God makes himself known again and again. Any attempt to interpret the once-for-allness of this event (the *Einmaligkeit*, the *ephapax* of the Christian faith) as depending on the unrepeatableness of a past event is bound to fail because this stresses only what the Christ event has in common with other historical events. It fails to see what makes it distinctive. For Bultmann, to speak of the *Einmaligkeit* of God's revelation in Christ is not to refer to the uniqueness of a past historical event (all such events are in a sense unique—they can never recur in the same time-space complex) but to point to the eschatological nature of this particular event which, while originating in a past happening, is always present in the proclamation of this as saving event.[38]

This view of the absoluteness of revelation raises two major issues.

(i) The first is the importance for Bultmann's thought of the uniqueness of God's act in Christ. Schubert Ogden, one of Bultmann's most sympathetic interpreters, persistently criticizes this feature of Bultmann's theology, claiming that it represents a basic structural inconsistency in his system. This criticism will be examined in more detail in the next chapter, but in the meantime we should note that as far as Bultmann's doctrine of revelation is concerned, far from indicating inconsistency it becomes the key to Bultmann's understanding of the absoluteness of revelation. Only in this way is he able to avoid extreme subjectivism. It could be, of course, that while it protects Bultmann at one point by providing a consistent view of revelation, it opens him at another point to the charge of inconsistency. Ogden claims that this is what has happened; according to him, this emphasis on the Christ event clashes with the existentialist reinterpretation of the gospel. To this wider criticism we will return later.

(ii) The second issue is the attention Bultmann gives (or fails to give) to the "historical Jesus." There can be no doubt that he wants to assert the ultimacy of the eschatological event, and to insist that this occurs only in the proclamation of the saving event in Christ. However, he insists also that the important feature is the repeatable nature of the salvation event rather than the unrepeatable precondition for the event—Jesus of Nazareth. And as part of his understanding of the hiddenness of God's revelation he denies that "historical research can ever encounter any traces of the epiphany of God in Christ."[39] I have no objection to this so long as he means that there is nothing about the life of Jesus that can *establish* this to the observer as the event of God's acting. But if he means that there *is* nothing significant about the life of Jesus for our understanding of God's revelation, then I cannot agree. Of course it takes an act of faith to discern in the life of Jesus the saving act of God, but this same faith hears more than the *that* of the event. The proclamation through which the eschatological event recurs has as its content not merely that God once acted and now acts, but that through the life and teaching of this particular man Jesus, portrayed as being one kind of man and not another, teaching this kind of thing about God and man and not something else, living this kind of life and not another, calling men to this kind of response and not another, the saving and revealing act of God becomes a present reality.

The debate about the relation between the kerygma and the historical Jesus will be taken up in the next chapter, but here it should be noted that unless Bultmann takes account of the content of this proclamation, he has not avoided the difficulty of subjectivism at all. If the absoluteness of God's revelation in Christ is based on the absolute nature of the decision that we must make when confronted with the kerygma, then there can still be an unlimited variety of interpretations of the revelation unless the content of the kerygma remains constant. This constancy is not provided if all that we can say is that the paradox of the Christian faith is its assertion that the historical event of Jesus of Nazareth becomes the eschatological event, for this still leaves the individual to imagine what he will about the nature and content of this event and of God's revelation. In answer to H. P. Owen's charge of subjectivism, Bultmann himself acknowledges that this is avoided only when it is recognized that "the Christian faith asserts that an historical event—that is Jesus' launching of his ministry, his activities and his fate—is the eschatological event."[40] The extent to which Bultmann's own method provides, or even allows for, a knowledge of Jesus' "ministry, activities and fate" will be discussed in the next chapter.

It may now be helpful to summarize what has been said about the absoluteness of Christian revelation.

Bultmann insists that the Christian revelation is absolute, but that its absoluteness is not that of timeless truth which can be recognized as such by the exercise of human reason. Nor is the Christian revelation "relatively absolute" in the sense of belonging to a religion superior to other religions.[41] Nor can this absoluteness be predicated upon the uniqueness and unrepeatableness of a past event in history, for this objectifies God's act and makes faith dependent upon a *historisch* relationship. Following his hermeneutical principle of concentrating on personal history rather than world history, Bultmann contends that the absoluteness of revelation inheres in the absoluteness of the decision with which man is confronted in the present as he hears the word of proclamation. Therefore, the *Einmaligkeit* of God's act in Jesus Christ lies not in the unrepeatable nature of the *historisch* Jesus of Nazareth but in the eschatological nature of the event that occurs through the proclamation of Jesus as the Christ.

Bultmann's insistence on the unique nature of God's saving and revealing act in Jesus Christ is an integral part of his attempt to retain the absoluteness of revelation without either locating this in an objectifiable event in the past or losing it in the plethora of individual interpretations. Whether this can be reconciled with his call for existential reinterpretation, and whether he gives sufficient attention to the content of the unique event, have yet to be discussed.

e. Revelation and creation

In an essay written in 1941,[42] Bultmann tackled the question of natural revelation. His conclusion that God does reveal himself in nature and history but that without Christ this is not revelation for us is neither original nor unorthodox. In fact, it echoes the Barmen Declaration of 1934, and, like it, had important implications not only for theology but for the question of how Christians should cope with life under the Nazi regime.[43] However, there is something original in the way Bultmann reached his conclusion, and since this reflects his preoccupation with the category of personal history and illustrates the reinterpretation of doctrine that results, it will be useful to see how his argument develops.

Bultmann begins by acknowledging that it is possible for anyone to have a general idea or a "concept" of God, and that there is a general consensus about the content of such a concept. This includes the characteristics of eternity, transcendence, omnipotence, and holiness. However, to have such a concept of God is not to have knowledge of him. It is possible to give content to the concept "unicorn" while knowing that there is no such animal. The concept of God becomes knowledge of God only when this carries conviction, that is, when it impinges upon my own self-understanding, when it affects how I see myself and how I live and act in consequence. Therefore, to know God as omnipotent is at the same time to recognize one's own powerlessness. To know him as judge is to acknowledge absolute demands upon onself. To know him as eternal is to be aware of one's own mortality.

> Knowledge about God is in the first instance a knowledge which man has about himself and his finitude, and God is reckoned to be the power which breaks through this finitude of man and thereby raises him up to his real nature.[44]

How is Christian belief related to this? Not, Bultmann says, by denying the validity of non-Christian inquiry about God, but by affirming that only Christian faith can provide the means of finding the answer. Apart from Christian revelation, there is no warrant for attributing omnipotence to God. God does not meet man as omnipotent will in either nature or history. Nor can man know that he stands under the demand of God apart from the revelation in Christ. Natural law does not point man beyond himself for the source of obligation he feels, nor can God's demand be known from history, because there is always another way of interpreting this. History is always ambiguous, and since its message is obscure, there is always risk in paying heed to it. And apart from Christ, all talk of God's eternity and transcendence is nothing more than an acknowledgment of man's ignorance and incapacity to speak of him.

The significance of the Christian revelation is that it now provides adequate grounds for affirming what were previously unsubstantiated aspects of a concept of God. In Jesus Christ, God is known as one whose revelation of himself is at the same time a word of grace and forgiveness to men. The event in which God discloses himself is at the same time one that frees man to see in God the Omnipotent, Holy, Eternal One. In this event, man is able to know God as omnipotent because the liberating power is known in his own life. In this event too God's holiness is taken seriously, for man's sin, while not glossed over as finitude or limitation, is overcome. Here too God's eternity is taken seriously because man knows life in a new dimension. Freed from the world and from bondage to its standards, man's own existence becomes eschatological, and he therefore knows the eternality of God:

> And so it is that Christian belief speaks of God's revelation in Christ as the forgiving grace of God by which he as the Omnipotent Holy Eternal One shows himself and thereby liberates man from himself, also teaching him to understand himself in his finitude and teaching him to understand God in his grace.[45]

Underlying this discussion of natural theology and the significance of Christian revelation is, of course, Bultmann's insistence upon the reciprocal relation between statements about God and statements about man. This is in turn based on his view of the centrality of *Geschichtlichkeit* in the structure of history,[46] so that insofar as God does reveal himself in history this is known only as he breaks into man's own historicity. So in this discussion of natural revelation, Bultmann supported his claim for the exclusiveness of Christian revelation by saying in effect that no talk about God apart from his revelation in Christ can reflect genuine knowledge of God. Only when man's own existence is shaped by God can he be said to know God, but since this occurs only through the act of God in Christ, all other attempts to speak of God are nonexistential and therefore do not speak of God's revelation at all. They can at best speak of man's lack of revelation.

A significant example of what happens when traditional doctrines are reformulated in line with this view of revelation is Bultmann's treatment of the doctrine of creation. Having made the distinction he does between *Natur* and *Geschichte*, insisting that theology must be relevant to the life of man in the world and must therefore find its place in the realm of history, Bultmann cannot allow a doctrine of creation to apply primarily in the realm of nature. Nor can he allow it to refer only to the origin of mankind in the world, for, to be genuinely theological, it must at the same time be significant for man's own existence in the present. So Bultmann makes the primary point of reference not the world or God as its source but the creatureliness of man:

> Only such statements about God are legitimate as express the existential relation between God and man. Statements which speak of God's actions as cosmic events are illegitimate. The affirmation that God is creator cannot be a theoretical statement about God as *creator mundi* in a general sense. The affirmation can only be a personal confession that I understand myself to be a creature which owes its existence to God.[47]

Therefore, Bultmann insists that the doctrine of creation refers to the historicity of man rather than to the origin of the cosmos. It is not a theory about the past but an affirmation about the present, showing man how he is now to understand himself. So Bultmann is able to insist that "faith in creation is the expression of a specific understanding of human existence."[48]

In an article written in 1936[49] that anticipates his 1941 treatment of natural revelation, Bultmann first indicates what this "specific understanding" is, acknowledging that this is in a sense already present in pre-Christian or non-Christian inquiry, but then affirming that only through faith in Christ does this understanding have existential impact and therefore theological validity. In most creation myths there is already evident the realization that man is an alien in the world, unable to establish for himself a place in the cosmic order. He knows that this place can be given to him only from a source that transcends the cosmos. However, without faith in Christ this knowledge is useless if not actually destructive, for without knowledge of the transcendent creator, man lives either in terror of the unknown or in false attempts to establish himself as part of the cosmos. In Christ, however, man is able to recognize his lostness for what it is, namely, a symptom of his sin, but at the same time he is able to hear the word of forgiveness and renewal that overcomes his sin. In Christ, therefore, the Creator-God is known at the same time to be the God of love who gives us our place in the cosmos. But this place is not a possession of ours which guarantees security; it is a stance of love toward the neighbor which has constantly to be renewed and thus to be realized (made real):

> This kind of a faith in creation is not a theory about some past occurrence such as might be depicted in mythological tales or cosmological speculation and natural scientific research; . . . rather it is an *existentiell* knowledge, i.e., a knowledge of myself as a rightwised sinner that has an effect on my existence and that must constantly be laid hold of anew.[50]

This way of interpreting the doctrine of creation has many advantages. To begin with, it bypasses the fruitless debate about whether faith in God as creator can be reconciled with the views of scientists about the origin of the world. At the same time it makes possible an interpretation of creation myths rather than a rejection of them or a purely formal retention as curios. It also faithfully reflects the New Testament recognition of the relation between God as creator and man as the new creation in Jesus Christ. Most significantly, I think, it enabled Bultmann to affirm the positive value of the world and its political and social structures, at the same time providing a basis from which to attack any attempt to give ultimate authority to such structures. He gave two extended answers to the question, What is the meaning of the doctrine of creation?[51] Each of these, written in the thirties, was also and obviously an answer to the question, How far can Christian allegiance to the state go? The answer was the same—Christian faith in God as creator demands that our participation in and use of the worldly powers is always limited. It depends upon

> our becoming clear ourselves and also seeing that no misunderstanding arises in the minds of others, that for us these powers are not ultimate powers, that beyond them stands the creative power of God that forbids us to fall down and worship them because all glory belongs to him as the creator.[52]

These were the words that needed to be spoken in Germany of the thirties, when unconditional support for the Nazi regime was being based on a view that argued from God as the creator to the word as his good creation, and then to the vital powers of the state as his presence in the world, demanding the totally committed support of his creatures. These are the words that need to be heard again in the sixties when governments in what we call democratic as well as totalitarian countries demand allegiance of a kind that allows no effective means of reservation or dissent, and when a theology of the secular which encourages men to respond to the call of God that comes from the world can easily be distorted into the same error of identifying particular movements and institutions unambiguously as God's work in the world, demanding total and uncritical commitment to them. This is not to say that God is not at work in secular movements and structures, nor that Christians should steer clear of them because they will inevitably be less than perfect and therefore embody evil as well as good, destructive as well as constructive potential. But it is to insist that belief in God as creator always has two implications. It shows us the value of human life and points to the world as the context within which we live the life God gives us. At the same time it sets limits to the authority of every worldly institution, freeing us to give absolute allegiance to God alone and opening our eyes to see that this allegiance is fulfilled only in love for others.

6
GOD'S ACT IN JESUS CHRIST

THERE CAN BE NO DOUBT that, for Bultmann, Christian faith comes into focus around the affirmation of God's decisive act in Jesus Christ. Although he may be criticized for the way he interprets this affirmation and he is often charged with inconsistency for continuing to stress its importance, his critics and his followers agree that his intention is to reaffirm the centrality of God's act in Christ. In the original essay on demythologizing, Bultmann rejected previous attempts because they failed precisely at this point. They eliminated the kerygmatic affirmation about this act of God. He, on the other hand, insisted that any interpretation of the New Testament witness must, if it is to be authentic, retain this affirmation as its central feature.[1] How does his own reinterpretation measure up to this demand?

a. The eschatological event

The term that Bultmann characteristically uses of God's act in Christ, viz., the eschatological event, itself indicates how his understanding of this act is shaped by his view of history. What he means by this has already been outlined in Chapter 2. For Bultmann, as I showed there, an eschatological event is one that transcends world history, having three defining features. First, its significance inheres primarily in the dimension of personal history. Second, though it occurs in world history and is to this extent visible, that it is *eschatological* is not apparent to empirical observation or research. Third, it is in the present that the event is of decisive importance for human existence.

Bultmann's understanding of Jesus Christ as eschatological

event is consistent at each point with this description. The significance of Christ transcends the dimension of world history. This is not to say that the eschatological event has no point of reference in the realm of world history. On the contrary, the act of God is indissolubly linked to a concrete historical person, Jesus of Nazareth, and this is the key to the kerygma. "Christian faith declares the paradox that an historical event (precisely, Jesus and his history) is at the same time an eschatological occurrence."[2] But while the event has this reference in world history, as eschatological it transcends this dimension.

In describing what transcendence means in this context, Bultmann employs the three defining features listed above. He insists first that Jesus Christ as eschatological event is significant primarily in the dimension of *Geschichtlichkeit*, so that the history that is brought to an end by God's act in Jesus Christ is personal history, and the world that is renewed is the "world" of man's own existence. The major achievement of the act of God is therefore the granting to man the possibility of new self-understanding.[3] Second, Jesus Christ can never be objectively identified as the eschatological event by observation, investigation, or research. Prior to the commitment of faith in which we receive from him the gift of new life we have no warrant for believing in Christ as the act of God. Apart from faith, the events of his life are indistinguishable from other events in world history.[4] Third, Jesus Christ is eschatological event only in the present, when he confronts men in their present situation with the possibility of new self-understanding. So Bultmann's way of dealing with the perennial problem of how a long-past occurrence can have any force in the present is to say that the event is renewed each time it is proclaimed and meets man in existential encounter.

Understanding Jesus Christ as eschatological event in this way has many doctrinal implications. To be consistent with this view, no statements about Christ are valid if they imply that he can be identified as the act of God by objective means, or that he is such as an event in the past, or that he is significant apart from existential response in the present. None of the traditional ways of speaking about Christ, e.g., as God, as Son of God, as God incarnate, as revelation of God, as salvation event, and so on, are acceptable unless they are translated out of the dimension of objective events in world history into the dimension of personal history in the present. Christological statements must therefore refer to the significance of Christ for our lives rather than to his nature or essential being. Just as affirmations about God must also be about our existence, so those concerning Jesus as the Christ must at the same time be about ourselves.[5] This does not mean that anthropological statements are to take the place of Christological ones, but that there must be a reciprocal relation between them.

This reinterpretation of statements about Jesus Christ may be consistent with Bultmann's view of history, of theology, and therefore of eschatological event, but is it consistent with the New Testament witness? It is not difficult to find many references there to the nature of Jesus Christ where the emphasis is on his relation to God, and where there appears to be no immediate implication for human existence. There are others who speak of him objectively and in terms of world-historical happenings. Still others claim quite explicitly to "establish him there and then as the Christ"[6] (although Bultmann claims that this is impossible) so that reader as well as eyewitness may come to believe. But Bultmann deals with these, as he does with other passages which do not cohere with his hermeneutical approach, by claiming that they represent only peripheral themes, whereas the dominant New Testament trends are consistent with his interpretation of eschatological event:

> In the New Testament at least *a parte potiori*, the pronouncements about Jesus' divinity or deity are not, in fact, pronouncements of his nature but seek to give expression to his significance; pronouncements which confess that what he says and what he is do not have their origin within the world, and are not human ideas nor events in the world, but that God speaks to us in them and acts towards us and for us. Christ is the power and wisdom of God; he became the wisdom of God, righteousness and sanctification and redemption for us

(I Cor. 1:30). So far then, I would say, as such pronouncements digress into objectivizing propositions, they are to be interpreted critically.[7]

This critical interpretation would presumably remove from further consideration passages that would otherwise tend to invalidate Bultmann's theological generalization.

Having sketched on broad canvas the way Bultmann's view of history and eschatological event influences his approach to the doctrine of Christ, we will now fill in some detail by considering three specific aspects of this doctrine, viz., of Christ as revelation of God, as God incarnate, and as salvation event.

(i) Attention has already been given to the consistency with which Bultmann applies his view of history to the understanding of Christ as revelation of God. It is not as an objectifiable event in the past that Christ reveals God. There is nothing about the past-historical happening as such that warrants its acceptance as revelation. This becomes revelation only when, through proclamation, it is renewed in the present and becomes decisively important in personal history as a means of self-understanding. Therefore, Christ did not reveal God either by living a life uniquely transparent to the being of God (to borrow Tillich's terminology), or by conveying through life and teaching certain ideas about him. He reveals God only by confronting us in the present with the possibility of new life, an offer only God can make and fulfill.[8] So, Bultmann holds, this revelation is absolute not because it is predicated upon the uniqueness of a past event, but because the decision that man must make when confronted with this event is of absolute significance to him.

(ii) Bultmann's view of the incarnation is similarly influenced by his understanding of history, and is consistent with the three defining features of eschatological event already discussed. This means that incarnation cannot be understood as an event in past history that can be identified as the act of God by observation. It can be understood only as an event in the present. So Bultmann affirms: "The incarnation is . . . an eschatological event and not a datable event of the past; it is an event which is continually being re-enacted in the event of the proclamation."[9] Therefore, when the Christian speaks about God's becoming man he should not intend to convey by this any eternal truths about the nature of God or of man or of the God-man. He should be referring instead to the fact that only in the word proclaiming Jesus Christ is man confronted with the eschatological event that reconstitutes his existence. According to Bultmann, what Christianity means by God's becoming man is that the reality of God's forgiveness and renewal in man's life is met with only in the word authenticated by Jesus Christ.[10] Throughout his essay on the Christological confession of the World Council of Churches,[11] Bultmann reiterates this contention that incarnation should be seen as event in the present, and in one passage, important enough to quote at length, he makes it clear that dominating the whole discussion is his view of Christ as eschatological event:

> Christ's lordship, his deity, is always only an event at any given time. Just this is the meaning of the statement that he is the Eschatological Event which can never be objectivized into an event of the past, nor into an event in a metaphysical sphere, which rather militates against every objectification. In this sense, therefore, it may be said that in him God is encountered. The formula "Christ is God" is false in every sense in which God is understood as an entity which can be objectivized. . . . It is correct if "God" is understood here as the event of God's acting.[12]

In this interpretation of the incarnation Bultmann has remained consistent with his view of history, and of the faith as historical, when he refuses to objectify the doctrine by locating its point of reference as a past-historical event. But in so doing, he clearly invites the charge of robbing the event of its uniqueness by allowing its repetition ad infinitum,[13] and of making man the effective agent of incarnation by having it occur only "where the Word of God wins its own acceptance in faith."[14] Can these charges be sustained?

There is no doubt that Bultmann does come dangerously close to saying that God becomes incarnate in Jesus Christ when, and only when, Jesus is recognized as the act of God, which implies that the incarnation is constituted by a human act of recognition. That this is not what he intends is shown by his insistence that Christ is the eschatological event when he is proclaimed as such, whether the response is positive or negative.[15] And it should also be recognized that Bultmann does not sever the connection between the incarnation, which occurs in the word of preaching, and the man Jesus of Nazareth, as the phrase "beginning with Jesus" in the following passage shows:

> The incarnation should not be conceived of as a miracle that happened about 1950 years ago, but as an eschatological happening which, beginning with Jesus, is always present in the words of men proclaiming it to be a human experience.[16]

Nevertheless, it cannot be denied that for Bultmann, God is incarnate not in the man Jesus but in the preaching about him. Therefore, while Bultmann does not say that the incarnation is dependent upon a favorable human response, he still implies that it is dependent upon human action, namely, proclamation. Without the word of preaching the incarnation does not occur.

This, it seems to me, reverses the priorities that should apply. I have no objection to the assertion that "God now confronts me in the word of preaching," and I agree that this is a result—in fact, the most significant result—of the incarnation. But I think Bultmann has stressed this consequence of the incarnation without giving appropriate place at all to the source and content of the Word—Jesus Christ. Using Bultmann's terms, what I want to say is that the eschatological event begins with Jesus himself, not merely in the sense of providing the prerequisite for preaching, but that in his life, in his recognition of his role as Messiah, in his obedient fulfilling of this role, and in his own teaching and proclamation Jesus *already* was the eschatological event. In this event, God had already turned toward the world. The church's proclamation, therefore, does not inaugurate the incarnation but reconstitutes the event in which God himself is acting.

(iii) I have been looking at examples of the way Bultmann's

view of eschatological event has shaped his doctrinal statements about Christ, and now come to his interpretation of Christ as salvation event. Again the influence of his view of history is evident, particularly in the way he understands the *extra nos* and *einmalig* character of this event.

The traditional way of understanding the *extra nos* aspect of God's saving work has been to see it as an event accomplished in the past without our knowledge or participation. Already in this past event evil was overcome and our salvation achieved. Preaching affirms that this saving event has already occurred in Christ and calls upon us to believe that this was done for us. Bultmann, however, can have none of this:

> *The salvation-occurrence is nowhere present except in the proclaiming, accosting, demanding, and promising word of preaching.* A merely "reminiscent" historical account referring to what happened cannot make the salvation occurrence visible. . . . Consequently, in the proclamation Christ himself, indeed God Himself, encounters the hearer, and the "Now" in which the preached word sounds forth is the "Now" of the eschatological occurrence itself.[17]

This passage and others like it make it clear that for Bultmann the salvation event is not *extra nos* in the traditional sense of an event that occurred in the past and that has objective saving efficacy apart from our response—indeed, apart even from our hearing of it. Is there any other way of understanding *extra nos?*

Bultmann claims that there is. His view implies that there can be no saving event outside the personal commitment of faith in the present moment. But it also implies that this commitment of faith is to something or someone coming to man from outside himself. It is true that for Bultmann there is no salvation event apart from the believer who receives his existence anew; it is equally true that this new existence is given to the believer by one who is other than himself. So Bultmann retains the *extra nos* element not by interpreting it as an occurrence that has saving efficacy independent of believing response, but by insisting that the salvation event is made possible only by God's *coming to* the believer, offering him eschatological existence. His own answer to the charge of dissolving the *extra nos* dimension is therefore a convincing one:

> We can make our answer . . . in the single affirmation that God meets us in His Word, in a concrete word, the preaching instituted in Jesus Christ. . . . This living Word of God is not invented by the human spirit and by human sagacity; it rises up in history.[18]

But is his answer to the parallel charge of having destroyed the once-for-all character of God's act in Christ equally convincing? This charge arises because Bultmann insists that the saving event is continually present in preaching, so that the "*ephapax* . . . does not mean the datable uniqueness and finality of an event of past history."[19] We have already faced the implications of this in relation to the doctrine of revelation, but it also has implications for the understanding of Christ's saving work. The most celebrated indictment of this aspect of Bultmann's views comes from Karl Barth, who claims that these amount to

> an existentialist translation of the sacramentalist teaching of the Roman Church, according to which, at the climax of the mass, with the transubstantiation of the elements . . . there is a "bloodless repetition" of the sacrifice of Christ on Golgotha.[20]

There is a good deal of truth in this. Bultmann's view of the re-presentation of the salvation event has definite sacrificial overtones. He acknowledges that in his view the kerygma offers not a *historisch* appropriation of the past but, "as a sacramental event, it re-presents the events of the past in such a way that it renews them."[21] He also agrees that the kerygma, like the sacraments, makes possible a present encounter in which the cross becomes an ever-present reality.

Does this mean that Barth's charge is sustained? Yes and no. It means that Barth has given an accurate description of Bultmann's view, but has not thereby shown what is wrong with it.

Of course, to demonstrate affinity with Roman Catholic views would, for some, be sufficient indictment in itself, and there is no doubt that Barth uses the terms "transubstantiation" and "bloodless sacrifice" in order to convey his own disapproval. However, polemics aside, what he has really shown is how firmly Bultmann stands within the Reformation tradition which looks for encounter with God in his word. The leaders of the Reformation also translated the Roman doctrine of the Mass; in so doing, they did not eliminate the view that in worship God continually comes to meet man. What they did was to change the locus of this encounter from the celebration of the Eucharist to the preaching of the word. It was this which led to the rebuilding of churches so that pulpits were located exactly where altars used to be, and to the restructuring of the liturgy so that the sermon came exactly at the place in worship formerly given to the elevation of the Host.

The parallel is not, of course, complete. While the Reformers did not deny that the saving event occurs again and again when men are confronted with the Word, they did deny that Christ's sacrifice could be repeated, either by word or sacrament. It is here that the polemical arrows that Barth fires at Bultmann are at their sharpest ("bloodless sacrifice," "transubstantiation"), but it is also here that they are widest from the mark, for it is just this idea of saving event as sacrifice that Bultmann proposes to demythologize. It hardly needs to be added that whereas the doctrine of transubstantiation has been taken to imply an objective sacrifice occurring independently of the response of the believer, nothing could be farther from Bultmann's understanding of eschatological event.

We have seen that for Bultmann belief in God's act in Jesus Christ, which occurs in the eschatological present, is the *sine qua non* of Christian faith. Two questions that have previously been raised must now be faced. First, is such a stress consistent with Bultmann's own project? Second, what is the relation between the present event of God's acting and the past life of Jesus of Nazareth? The first will be discussed now, the second in Sec. c.

b. Demythologizing and the Christ event

As Macquarrie has shown, at least two different lines of criticism converge at this point.[22] Some theologians who want to emphasize the importance of God's having acted in history think that Bultmann's approach leaves no ground for such an emphasis. Others, who want to be rid of this stress on God's act in history because they see it as a remnant of mythology, think that Bultmann should have done this himself by applying his own principles consistently. But both agree that Bultmann, while in fact claiming that it is essential to stress God's act, has no warrant in his theological method for making this emphasis.

Karl Barth has recognized the "criticism which Bultmann has received at this point from right and from left,"[23] and, agreeing that Bultmann does leave himself open to the charge despite "the emphasis which he lays upon the character of the deed as history," identifies himself with the right-wing critics by expressing the wish that Bultmann would give a historical grounding in the cross and resurrection for his emphasis on the Christ event. Markus Barth follows the same line in his essay "Introduction to Demythologizing," agreeing that there is a basic inconsistency in Bultmann's system between the principles and "the way by which he is attempting to carry out his program."[24] But he claims that it is this very inconsistency which allows Bultmann to remain a theologian and a Christian! Macquarrie too, while claiming that the decisive act of God in Christ must be retained, says that this cannot be done while holding consistently to Bultmann's view that all theological statements must be understood in terms of human existence. According to Macquarrie, as soon as we speak of God's act in Jesus Christ we are making or implying statements that are not statements about human existence, and have therefore "abandoned the concept of a purely existential theology."[25] He concludes that we ought therefore to abandon the attempt to follow a purely existential method in theology.

A contrary proposal comes from the so-called "critics on the left." They agree that to speak of an act of God is to abandon existential theology. Therefore, they say, retain existential theology but abandon statements about an act of God in history. So Fritz Buri,[26] claiming that Bultmann's inconsistency arises from his attempt to retain the kerygmatic emphasis on God's act while calling for a demythologizing whose principles logically imply rejection of such an emphasis as patently mythological, insists that the only solution is to "dekerygmatize," i.e., to eliminate the appeal to an *event* of salvation. Schubert Ogden, who takes a similar line, agrees that Bultmann cannot retain reference to God's decisive act in Jesus Christ without denying the basic elements of demythologizing. He insists that if the project were carried through consistently, Bultmann's contention that salvation is achieved only through a unique act of God in history could not be sustained.[27] This would then break down Bultmann's distinction between philosophy and theology,[28] would remove the claim that authentic human existence is possible solely in consequence of God's act in Christ, and would open the way for a theology oriented toward process philosophy rather than existentialism. Ogden sees himself as carrying through this project consistently.[29]

Despite the different perspective and the contrary proposals, the criticism from both sides amounts to the same thing—that Bultmann is inconsistent when he proposes demythologizing on the one hand and retaining the kerygmatic stress on God's act in Christ on the other. Is he inconsistent in this way?

Yes, if he is held to the broad definition of myth given in the original essay. In that essay he defined myth as "the use of imagery to express the otherworldly in terms of this world and the divine in terms of human life."[30] If rigidly applied, this does mean that any talk at all about a God who transcends this world will be mythological, including talk of his act in Jesus Christ. But since it was never Bultmann's intention to eliminate expressions that are mythological in this broad sense, he revised his references to myth to make it clear that the New Testament expressions that are the target of demythologizing are those which objectify the divine and otherworldly. By "objectify" he means speaking of the divine or otherworldly in such a way that its transcendent character is lost by becoming simply a spectacular feature of this world. An extended quotation from Bultmann will serve to recapitulate the discussion in Chapter 4, Sec. c, on myth and objectification:

> Mythological thought regards the divine activity, whether in nature or history, as an interference with the course of nature, history, or the life of the soul, a tearing of it asunder—a miracle, in fact. Thus it objectifies the divine activity and projects it on to the plane of worldly happenings. A miracle —i.e. an act of God—is not visible or ascertainable like worldly events. The only way to preserve the unworldly, transcendental character of the divine activity is to regard it not as an interference in worldly happenings, but something accomplished *in* them in such a way that the closed weft of history as it presents itself to objective observation is left undisturbed.[31]

Another way of making the same point would be to say, following my analysis of the structure of history as Bultmann sees it, that demythologizing is aimed at those expressions which locate the divine activity in the dimension of *Weltgeschichte* and assert that there is something about this act which enables *historisch* observation to identify it as God's act. Demythologizing accepts the intention of these mythological expressions (which is to point to that which transcends human existence), but proposes to fulfill this intention by speaking of the act of God in a way that does not locate this in *Weltgeschichte* or allow it to be identified as God's act by *historisch* observation. It is just this purpose that Bultmann seeks to achieve by speaking of God's act in Jesus Christ as the "eschatological event," and we have already concluded in Chapter 6, Sec. a, above that he does this in such a way that the event is not located in past world history open to *historisch* investigation, but is decisively significant in the present for human existence. In other words, Bultmann's way of speaking about Christ as eschatological event does not contravene his own demythologizing proposal as long as his revised definition of myth as "objectification" is accepted. Where does this leave him in relation to the specific charges of inconsistency that are leveled against him?

(i) It must be recognized at the outset that Bultmann's overriding concern is to find a way of explicating the New Testament kerygma that Jesus Christ is Lord, and that therefore the demythologizing project sought from the beginning to speak of God's act in Christ in a nonobjectivizing way.[32] It is therefore quite misleading to suggest, as Henderson does, that Bultmann got the project going independently of this concern, and then foundered and plunged into inconsistency because he was not able, or was finally reluctant, to demythologize the act of God. It is just not true that when he comes to the action of God through Jesus Christ, Bultmann "calls a halt to the process of demythologizing."[33] In a way that is quite consistent with his more careful definition of myth outlined above, Bultmann does demythologize the act of God by speaking of this as the eschatological event that is of decisive significance in the dimension of *Geschichtlichkeit*. This complies with his own requirements for demythologizing, namely, by referring to the act of God in a way that does not objectify this either by locating it in past world history or by making it identifiable as God's act by *historisch* research. Bultmann's right-wing critics may still insist that this way of understanding the historicity of God's act is unacceptable because it stresses personal rather than world history. However, they are not justified in asserting that Bultmann, in retaining the stress on God's act as he does, is being inconsistent with the principles of demythologizing as he has set them down.

(ii) Ogden's charge of inconsistency is more subtle than Henderson's, but just as misleading. Bultmann's continued stress on the act of God is inconsistent, according to Ogden, not so much with the demythologizing principles as such as with the whole thrust of Bultmann's existential theology. Bultmann's intention is to undertake a thoroughgoing existentialist interpretation of theological statements. This means, according to Ogden, that

> Christian faith is to be interpreted exhaustively and without remainder as man's original possibility of authentic historical (*geschichtlich*) existence as this is more or less adequately clarified and conceptualized by an appropriate philosophical analysis.[34]

Therefore (so Ogden's argument runs), when Bultmann claims that the transition from inauthentic to authentic existence is achieved through the unique act of God in Christ, this violates the existentialist principle of speaking only of man's existence because it speaks about an act of God in space and time.

The misleading thing about this argument is that nowhere does Bultmann imply that by "existentialist interpretation" he means what Ogden says he means. Nowhere does he set out to interpret Christian faith into statements about man's historical existence "without remainder." In fact, from the beginning he insists that man's authentic historical existence, which may be described by some philosophies (particularly those with existentialist orientation), cannot be realized apart from the Christ event. While Bultmann insists that speaking about God must, at the same time, be speaking about human existence, he does not suggest that existential interpretation means a reduction of the former into the latter, a "translation without remainder." Again the charge of inconsistency fails. By continuing to speak of the decisive act of God in Christ, Bultmann may fail to satisfy Ogden's requirements for existential reinterpretation, but he does not contravene his own.

(iii) Another of Ogden's criticisms is appropriate here, particularly because it seems to overlook one of the main aspects of Bultmann's view of history. Ogden claims that, according to Bultmann, "Christian faith is actually realizable, or is a 'possibility in fact' only because of the particular historical (*historisch*) event of Jesus of Nazareth."[35] Therefore theology must speak about

> a unique act of God in the person and destiny of Jesus of Nazareth which, as [Bultmann] says "first makes possible" the authentic human existence that philosophy also knows about and proclaims as man's original possibility.[36]

Ogden concludes that consistent demythologizing would remove this reference to God's act, and that the difference between theology and philosophy would disappear, since they both interpret man and his possibility in the same way.

Bultmann's 1941 essay might have led to this kind of conclusion, but not his writings since then. In this later writing, it becomes clear that it is not, as Ogden contended, the "person and destiny of Jesus of Nazareth" that is the act of God. As Bultmann makes quite clear in opposition to Buri, it is not in the person and destiny of Jesus that the unique act of God is manifest, but in his becoming the eschatological event decisive for personal history. Bultmann agrees that God's creative operation is not confined to the historical personality of Jesus when this is understood as an "objectifiable historical phenomenon." However, he insists that it is so confined when "the historical person Jesus of Nazareth is understood as the Eschatological Event which is present in the Word of preaching at any given time."[37] So Ogden is mistaken when he interprets Bultmann as locating the decisive act of God in the *historisch* event of Jesus of Nazareth, for Bultmann actually locates this in Christ as eschatological event, present not in *Weltgeschichte* but in *Geschichtlichkeit* through the word of preaching.

This also shows that Bultmann's theology-philosophy separation is due to more than an inconsistent clinging to a *historisch* happening, and this points to a second weakness in Ogden's estimate of the demythologizing project. Bultmann contends not only that philosophy (including existential philosophy) cannot achieve authentic human existence but that it cannot have full knowledge of it either. As he says in his reply to Schniewind: "We can know the true nature of eschatological existence only through God's revelation of himself in Christ. Our previous knowledge of it was but ignorance or error."[38] While it is possible to have an understanding of existence in philosophy apart from the eschatological event, this is still not equivalent to a Christian understanding, because it is not knowledge of eschatological existence. Therefore, the distinction Bultmann draws between theology and philosophy is not accurately described by saying that both recognize what authentic existence is, but only theology speaks of the act through which it is realized. According to Bultmann, even in looking at what authentic existence *is*, philosophy is at fault because it sees man capable of achieving this himself. This is not just a false idea about the way of achieving such life but is a false view of authentic existence itself, for it fails to see the source and limits of such existence lying outside man himself. This failure to recognize the boundaries distorts the whole picture.

I have said that at vital points Ogden's interpretation of Bultmann is inaccurate and therefore misleading. I believe that this is due not to any lack of appreciation for Bultman on Ogden's part but, on the contrary, to a desire to stay with Bultmann long after his own philosophical preferences and theological conclusions should have led him to break away. Ogden's philosophical orientation is toward process philosophy. His theological preference is to begin with the doctrine of God set in the context of philosophical theology, and to reach conclusions about the uniqueness or otherwise of God's act in Christ from that perspective. In each of these stances he is fundamentally at odds with Bultmann, who begins with the Biblical affirmation of God's act in Christ and seeks to understand both God and human existence from that perspective, making use of existentialist philosophy where this seems appropriate. I think, therefore, that Ogden's own theology would be clearer if he relied less on his interpretation of Bultmann to shore it up, and his criticisms of Bultmann would certainly be more cogent if he made them from an independent theological perspective, rather than by suggesting that they come from within Bultmann's system and therefore reveal a basic inconsistency within that system.

(iv) Now a briefer note on Macquarrie's version of Bultmann's inconsistency. In *An Existentialist Theology,* Macquarrie asserts that to speak of an act of God is necessarily to abandon existential theology.[39] This would be true if such a statement did not, at the same time, say something about human existence. However, as we have seen, this is just what Bultmann's interpretation seeks to do—to speak of the act of God not in and for itself but only as it is significant for the existence of man. There is no need to enlarge on this any further because, in his later book *The Scope of Demythologizing,* Macquarrie modifies his view to some extent, saying that what he formerly saw as an inconsistency in Bultmann's method that seriously limited its capacity to communicate the gospel he now recognizes as a genuine reflection of the paradox of the Christian faith.[40] However, while Macquarrie might be convinced about this, Bultmann would not. In the first place, Bultmann would argue, with justification I believe, that there is no inconsistency in his system of the kind that Macquarrie alleges. To speak of an act of God may contravene the existentialist views of some and the demythologizing aspirations of others, but it is inconsistent with neither of these as Bultmann has defined them. In the second place, the paradox of the Christian faith as Bultmann sees it is not, as Macquarrie suggests, that God acts in history at all. It is that he acts in an event which, to all outward intents and purposes, is an ordinary everyday event. The paradox is not that God acts, but that his act is hidden in the life of a man, so that a historical event is, at the same time, the eschatological event.

c. *The historical Jesus*

What relation does Bultmann see between the eschatological act of God that occurs in present historicity and the past-historical life of Jesus of Nazareth? Some attention has already been given to this. In Chapter 2, Sec. a, it was shown that Bultmann does insist upon retaining the relationship between the past and the present events. In Chapter 4, Sec. c, where it was argued that in translating the gospel along existentialist lines Bultmann does retain the kerygmatic stress on the eschatological event, the question between the relation of this event to the past history of Jesus of Nazareth was left in abeyance. In Chapter 5, Sec. b, it was argued that Bultmann does not do justice to the *geschichtlich* dimension of the Synoptic proclamation, and so fails to recognize that very often the New Testament writers invite response to God's act precisely by pointing to the past events of Jesus' life. And in Chapter 5, Sec. d, it was shown that the question of the relation between eschatological event and Jesus of Nazareth is of paramount importance in evaluating Bultmann's view of revelation, because this view leads to subjectivism unless some content is given to the present encounter in which revelation occurs. These various strands should now be drawn together.

Bultmann is persistently criticized for severing all links with past history, for destroying the historical basis of the faith, for ignoring the relation between our present life and the past life of Christ, and for fabricating a theology of existence as a substitute for the historical faith that his critical method destroyed. Whatever the variations on this critical theme, the keynote comes through clearly enough, viz., that even if Bultmann does still speak of a saving act of God, he nevertheless severs the relationship between this event and the past event of Jesus, so destroying the historical basis of Christianity. Is this a valid criticism?

There can be no doubt that Bultmann consistently repudiates the view that Christian faith can be established on the basis of a past-historical occurrence. But he does not mean by this that happenings in the past are irrelevant for faith, nor that Christian faith could exist now without Jesus of Nazareth then, nor that the kerygma could exist independently of the past event of the cross. He acknowledges that severing the link between present faith and past event of Christ (which never was his intention) would destroy the kerygma,[41] and recently he has insisted again that there can be no existential interpretation of the faith without adherence to the past event of Christ.[42] What he does mean is that although God has acted in an event in the past, *that* God was acting there cannot be deduced by any *historisch* approach to that event. It is in this sense, therefore, that Bultmann says that "faith, being personal decision, cannot be dependent upon a historian's labor."[43] This does not mean that there was no act, nor that the historian can tell us nothing about the event. It does mean that, whatever the historian tells us, this can give no support to the affirmation that here God was acting, and just this is the scandal of the Christian faith. This scandal, that the claim of faith cannot be verified by historical investigation, Bultmann seeks at all costs to preserve.

This refusal of Bultmann to allow faith to be shored up by

historical conclusions means that the relation between present saving event and past life of Jesus cannot be that of historical re-presentation. Such a relation is excluded also by his demythologizing principles, which, as we have seen, prohibit God's act from being located in past world history and from being independent of human response. Bultmann therefore says that the act of God which is the saving event occurs in the present word of proclamation and nowhere else. This act originates in the kerygma of the church about the "concrete historical man" Jesus of Nazareth, and is continually renewed in the preaching that confronts us in the present. For Bultmann, therefore, it is not only impossible to get behind the testimony of the early church to see what Jesus was really like, it is also quite irrelevant, because God reveals himself in the present encounter with the preaching about Christ and not in the past-historical Jesus at all. It is only Jesus Christ as he is preached and not the historical Jesus who is the Lord.[44] He becomes the eschatological event in the preaching which meets with faith or unbelief in the present.[45] So, Bultmann's answer to the question of the relation between the eschatological act of God in the present and the past life of Jesus is that in the event of preaching and response, Christ becomes the eschatological event.

This way of referring to the act of God, while retaining some links with the past and remaining consistent with the principles of demythologizing, seems to me to be defective in at least three ways.

First, it tends to compound the old error of separating the Jesus of history from the Christ of faith. While the purpose for stressing the distinction, which is to make it clear that *historisch* observation does not make Jesus visible as the Christ of God, may be laudable, Bultmann's way of doing this does leave him open to the charge of giving a new version of the old heresy of dividing the person of Christ.[46]

Second, it does tend to leave devoid of content the revelation of God which occurs in the eschatological event, thus inviting the individual believer to provide his own by some kind of private and direct communication, and consequently opening the way to a riot of subjective interpretations. Again, the purpose is sound; Bultmann is right to insist that the revelation of God is not open to verification by historical research. But why does he go on to conclude that: "Jesus as the Revealer of God reveals nothing but that he is the revealer"; and that "John . . . in his Gospel presents only the fact (*das Dass*) of the Revelation without describing its content,"[47] so that the revelation of God properly understood is "God speaking directly to me"?[48] By pressing his point as far as that, Bultmann jeopardizes his whole attempt to establish the absoluteness of God's act on grounds other than its location in the past.

Third, it tends to locate God's act within the preaching about Jesus as the Christ without acknowledging that the event began with Jesus himself.[49] Once again, the purpose, which is to avoid confining God's act to a past occurrence, is clear enough, but is it then necessary to imply, as Bultmann does, that the incarnation originated in Jesus Christ only in the sense that he later became the subject of the church's preaching, i.e., that in that preaching he became incarnate?

These defects—namely, the separation of the Jesus of history from the Christ of faith, the lack of content in God's revelation and the consequent danger of extreme subjectivism, and the locating of incarnation within the church's preaching rather than in the person of Jesus—seem to me to be so serious that they call Bultmann's whole system into question. If they necessarily follow from Bultmann's method, then, despite its other advantages, I would feel obliged to abandon his method of approach. However, I believe that although Bultmann himself runs into these dangers, it is still possible to avoid them while staying largely within his system.

I think, for instance, that it is entirely possible to give content to the revelation of God in Christ using a historical approach that does not run counter to Bultmann's own principles. Some of his followers who have engaged in what is sometimes called the "new quest" have shown how this is possible,[50] and although Bultmann has criticized their efforts, I find his criticism, for the most part, unconvincing. These attempts all begin by accepting

Bultmann's assertions that it is impossible by *historisch* investigation to get behind the New Testament proclamation in order to find out "exactly what happened," and that any attempt to build up faith by proving that the facts of Jesus' life warrant belief in him as the Christ is actually destructive of such faith. But they do not accept Bultmann's conclusion that nothing more can be known and nothing more should be sought concerning what Jesus reveals except that he is the revealer. So they approach the New Testament in various ways, expecting that by their efforts the one to whom the kerygma points will emerge more clearly, not because they hope to distinguish the Jesus of history from the Christ of faith whom the early church proclaimed, but because they want to see more clearly what the church was proclaiming about this Christ of faith.

It seems to me that this kind of approach does not contravene Bultmann's basic theological orientation at all. It is not a reversion to the attempt to write a *historisch* account of the life of Jesus; it is an attempt to see more clearly what the New Testament writers believed and proclaimed about Jesus as the Christ. It is not an attempt to validate the faith by showing that there are adequate historical facts about Jesus to warrant faith, because even when the New Testament picture of Jesus is clarified the question whether we believe what is claimed for him can be answered only in faith. It is still the question whether in the present proclamation the same saving event occurs in my history as was said to have occurred in the history of the first believers. Such an approach also recognizes (in a way that Bultmann often fails to do) that the Synoptic Gospels, as well as Paul and John, are designed to provide a *geschichtlich* account of the Jesus event, so that what emerges as they are considered more closely is a figure who precipitates existential decision. Deciding about him is at the same time deciding about ourselves. Therefore, if Bultmann's own basic hermeneutical principle is applied—namely, to approach the text with the question that the authors had foremost in mind—then the Synoptic Gospels challenge us to accept their answer not to the question, What happened? but to the questions, Who is he and who am I? This is clearly the existential question which precipitates the response of faith, the response in which one's own being is at stake and is reconstituted if the response is positive; and it seems to me absurd to expect such a reorientation of life in response to the Christ event unless the proclamation of that event has enough content to show the direction such a new orientation should take.

In 1962, Bultmann undertook to evaluate the work of scholars who were engaged in the kind of task I have just outlined,[51] and on the whole he was critical of their attempts. He acknowledges that there is at one level an indispensable continuity between the kerygma and the historical Jesus because the kerygma is about the historical Jesus. It therefore presupposes the Jesus of history. But does it go beyond the "that" of his history to the "what and how"? As he sees it, that is the point at issue between himself and his followers. He begins by asserting that nothing more is needed, and that Paul and John, each in his own way, show that nothing more than the "that" is needed. Paul provides no portrait of Christ apart from the cross, and this is seen not from a biographical standpoint but as saving event. And while John emphasizes the humanity of Jesus, he does not do so by offering historical facts from his life as the Synoptics do.[52] However, Bultmann persists with the question of whether, although it is not necessary for faith, there nevertheless is continuity in content, and acknowledges that from the Gospels certain factual conclusions about Jesus' work can be reached, e.g., that he broke with the Jewish law, performed exorcisms, enjoyed fellowship with outcasts, called followers, and so on. But he goes on to insist that none of these details proves that the kerygmatic conclusion about Jesus was justified.

So far, of course, Bultmann has said nothing that cuts across the approach of his followers outlined above. His argument does not touch those who assert that in order to know what kind of response the kerygma elicits, there must be content to the proclamation, i.e., that the kerygma can be eschatological only when the call to new self-understanding gives shape to that understanding, and can be Christian only when that shape is a reflection of what the kerygma says about Jesus. However, he then goes on to consider in turn the efforts of a number of his followers, and dismisses them one by one. Fuchs, he claims, abandons the existential approach by falling into a historicopsychological interpretation. Ebeling, by stressing the witness of faith, Bornkamm, by retaining a "twilight interest" in the church's actual memory, and Käsemann, by trying to delineate the peculiarity of Jesus' mission, all, according to Bultmann, abandon the existential venture by returning to the haven of bases that can be established and protected by historicocritical methods. Only Braun, who reduces the various kerygmatic forms to aspects of man's self-understanding before God, and Robinson, who shows the identity of the work of Jesus with the kerygma in placing man before the same decision, receive his commendation.

Why is Bultmann so critical of these attempts? His reluctance to engage in the new quest, or even to give it his support, is partly due to his own research into how the gospel tradition has been used in the formation of the New Testament. According to his view,[53] isolated sayings were molded into a gospel through the invention of appropriate "historical" settings for these sayings, so that from the Gospels only minimal knowledge of the actual events of Jesus' life can be gained. This, however, is not a compelling reason to boycott the new quest, for this aims at clarifying the portrait of Jesus painted in the kerygma; it is not really concerned to establish what the man who was the subject of that portrait was actually like.

Bultmann's other reason is the more important one. He claims that the attempt to establish content continuity between the historical Jesus and the church's kerygma is to abandon the existential approach and thus to lose the possibility of genuine faith encounter with the kerygma. Of course he is right to dismiss, as destructive as well as futile, attempts to construct a *historisch* image of Jesus. But he fails to acknowledge the importance of delineating the New Testament portrait of Christ precisely because it is this which precipitates and gives form to our faith response. And part of that faith response is that what the New Testament proclaims about Jesus is true. There is certainly no way of proving its truth by *historisch* means, but this is not the intention of any of the men Bultmann criticizes. They are simply affirming that faith accepts as true what cannot be historically verified, and that a *geschichtlich* approach to the New Testament shows this truth to be not just *that* Jesus is revealer but also *what* his life reveals. Bultmann's own conclusion about the Synoptics is that they do not intend to describe "just what happened," but rather to "give legitimacy to the history of Jesus as Messianic history, as it were, by viewing it in the light of kerygmatic Christology."[54] It is therefore difficult to see why he objects to the kind of *geschichtlich* approach to the Synoptics which such an estimate of their intention invites.

What I have been saying in the last few paragraphs amounts to this: Bultmann retains the historical connection between the past fact of Jesus and the present saving event. However, this is reduced to the bare fact *that* in Jesus Christ, God revealed himself and acted for our redemption, with no content being given to that event from the life of Jesus. Nevertheless, Bultmann's own view of the Synoptics as kerygmatic history, of Paul and John as inviting *geschichtlich* response, and of faith as occurring in existential response to the kerygma and not as a result of *historisch* research, all open the way to an approach to the New Testament which he might have adopted but did not. This approach would give content to the revelation by clarifying how the believing community understood Jesus, and would invite present commitment to the same understanding that includes self-understanding. It is this possibility, consistent with his own basic approach despite his protests to the contrary, which is being followed by a number of his students; and this, I believe, overcomes one of the most serious weaknesses in his own conclusions.

Earlier in this section I indicated what seem to me to be serious defects in Bultmann's view of God's act in Christ, but also said that these do not necessarily follow from his own hermeneutical principles and his view of history. The preoccupation of some of his followers with the figure of Christ in the Gospels was given as an extended example. I shall now suggest another way of understanding the act of God in Christ which, while remaining consistent with Bultmann's basic approach, overcomes some of the main defects in his conclusions.

d. A *constructive alternative*

The key to this alternative is found in Friedrich Gogarten's insistence that the act of God originates not in the kerygma about Jesus, nor in the "nature" of Jesus as a past-historical personality, but in the proclamation of Jesus himself. It is in Jesus' own proclamation that God turns toward man directly, once and for all.[55] This means that the Word of God is incarnate primarily in the word that Jesus proclaims, and subsequently in the church's witness to him: "When it is asserted that the Word of Jesus is the Word of God this means that in this Word, by Jesus speaking it, the same thing happens as happens if God speaks."[56] This way of looking at the act of God does not objectify it according to Bultmann's use of the term "objectify." It does not locate and confine it to a past-historical happening independent of human apprehension nor speak of it in a way that makes verification by historical research possible. Only through our hearing the word in faith does this become an event in which God turns to *us*, and only by faith do we accept the New Testament kerygma as an authentic reflection of the word that Jesus proclaimed.

In this context the historical Jesus is seen to be of primary significance, for it is no other than this man whom God sends into the world to proclaim his word. In his obedient assent to the role God assigned him, in his speaking the word given him by God rather than his own, and in his recognition and proclamation of himself as the saving event, Jesus was the Christ and himself constitutes the saving act of God. Whereas Bultmann says that Jesus becomes the eschatological event in the church's proclamation, I would want to say that this is true only because first he became the eschatological event by his own obedient hearing, proclaiming, and living of the word given to him by God. I would agree, of course, that what this word was, and that

Jesus spoke, lived, and died in obedience to that word, cannot be established by historical research. It comes only through faithful hearing of the New Testament kerygma.

Following this alternative would not contravene Bultmann's demythologizing principles by objectivizing the act of God either by confining it to the past or by implying that it can be known as God's act by historical research. Although God's act is here seen as already constituted by Jesus and his word, it is by no means confined to the past, but occurs whenever the kerygma is proclaimed and finds response. And while here it is the life of Jesus which provides the unique occasion for our encounter with God, it is still this life as proclaimed in the kerygma, and not any account that claims to lay bare the *historisch* facts, in which God meets us. While the redemptive act is seen to originate in the past occurrence, this does not become the eschatological event apart from faithful recognition of the life of Jesus as the act of God.

How would this emphasis modify Bultmann's conclusions?

(i) In the first place, this way of employing Bultmann's own basic ideas minimizes the danger of bifurcating the person of Jesus Christ. Amos wrote about a man who ran away from a bear in the desert only to be bitten by a snake when he thought he was safe at home. Something like this can happen to those who, like Bultmann, run so energetically away from every attempt to make faith dependent upon the results of historical research. They are then in danger of relying on an event in some esoteric kind of history that has no real relation to happenings in history at all. Having escaped the bear of historicism, they may be bitten by the snake of Docetism. Recognizing this danger, Gogarten meets it head-on, saying of God's act in Christ:

> One must not understand this coming of God as something suprahistorical, because the Christian faith stands or falls with the fact that God's coming encounters us in quite a peculiar sense in the historical life of the man Jesus of Nazareth, and not apart from it. . . . To believe on him means to recognize in the history of this one man our own history and that of all others, and then to receive the possibility of exposing ourselves, in union with him, to the future of God.[57]

This means that the "Jesus of history" "Christ of faith" distinction can be retained only as reflecting two different methods of approach to the documents that refer to the life of Jesus. It is possible to distinguish history as experienced by faith and as viewed by reason. Nevertheless, they are not two separate histories, and the Christ who is experienced by faith is no other than the Jesus who lived in history.

So far, this point has been put negatively by saying that the approach suggested by a key idea from Gogarten avoids the danger that Bultmann runs into of dividing Christ's person. Put positively, the approach provides a way of speaking about the unity of the human and the divine in Christ without reverting to metaphysical speculation about "essence" and "nature." I have already suggested that instead of saying with Bultmann that Jesus becomes the eschatological event through the church's proclamation, we should say that he becomes this through his own obedient hearing, proclamation, and living of the word of God. If this suggestion is followed, we can then interpret the unity of Christ not metaphysically but historically, not in terms of two natures but of identification of Jesus with both the will of God and the needs of man. The obedient hearing and response of Jesus to the Father achieves his unity with God and with man. This is not then a unity of essence, but a unity effected within history by the action of "that one man Jesus Christ," a unity that has its locus not (in metaphysical terms) in the nature of man but in his obedience to the word of God.

This way of looking at the person of Christ may well draw the charge of Monothelitism. However, such a label is appropriate only in the context of essentialist categories, where "unity of will" is something different from "unity of essence" because there will is seen as only one aspect of the essential person. But where existentialist categories are employed, as they are here, will or decision are not simply aspects among others of a person; they are constitutive of who that person is. They are precisely what makes a man the person he is and not someone different. To say in this context that "Jesus' unity of will with the Father is achieved through his obedience" is not to say that at only one point is he at one with God; it is to say that at *the* one point which makes him who he is, he is at one with God.

(ii) A second implication now becomes apparent. If the redemptive event is already constituted in Jesus' own proclamation, then the teaching of Jesus, particularly his teaching about himself, has a status not afforded it by Bultmann. He insists that the New Testament kerygma is not based on the teachings of Jesus, which can be subsumed under the heading "Judaism," and that the form in which they appear in the New Testament was dictated not by historicobiographical interest but by the need to regulate the conduct of believers and to keep their hopes alive.[58] However, while it is true that much of Jesus' teaching is found within Judaism, one important feature is not, namely, his teaching about himself. It is on this teaching which reflects Jesus' recognition of and obedience to the role assigned him by God that the kerygma is based. If it is, as I have argued, by this act of obedience that Jesus' word and the Word of God are one, then Jesus' teaching about himself is of primary importance. In particular, the question of the self-consciousness of Jesus is seen to have theological significance and is not, as Bultmann contends, to be dismissed as theologically irrelevant.[59]

Why does Bultmann reach this conclusion about Jesus' self-consciousness? In his early discussion of form criticism, he held that the discussion of this question was "perfectly futile,"[60] not because the question was insignificant but because the existence of so many opposing opinions shows that historical research can never hope to settle the question. Nevertheless, he inclines to the view that Jesus never saw himself as Messiah at all, but became such in the faith of the community.[61] In his *Theology of the New Testament* he goes farther, insisting that no such *historisch* fact could be an article of faith even if it were established, and concludes that the whole matter should be dismissed as a *historische Frage* with no significance for theology. So his argument runs: Historical research cannot establish the Messianic consciousness of Jesus because there is insufficient evidence available, and what there is tends to suggest that he did not see himself this way at all. In any case, the question is irrelevant for faith, since faith can never be founded upon historical investigation. Against that argument, I propose the following: Historical investigation cannot establish the self-consciousness of Jesus because insufficient evidence is available and because this is an article of faith which cannot depend for its verification upon historical research, but that Jesus was conscious of his Sonship is part of the affirmation of faith that in his obedient speaking God's word was being proclaimed.

I agree, therefore, with John McIntyre when he says that a first point in our Christology must be that Jesus Christ himself should be aware of that revelation of which he was the bearer.[62] Without this awareness there is no basis for speaking of Christ's obedience, which is the focal point of Christology for me, as I think it should be for any who take Bultmann's existentialist approach seriously. To put this another way: If we agree to use Bultmann's historicoexistentialist categories rather than essentialist ones, we shall not talk about incarnation in terms of nature and essence. A person is his history, not his nature. But then, on Bultmann's own terms, how a man understands himself is of decisive significance for who he is. Therefore, Jesus' self-understanding is of major importance because it is constitutive of who he is. This means that whether my conclusions about his self-consciousness are valid or not, still the question of his self-consciousness is a theologically relevant one. It is significant for faith and should not be brushed aside as merely a *historische Frage*.

(iii) A third implication of this alternative proposal is that the Gospel accounts of Jesus' life gain greater revelatory significance. This is so, not because they provide biographical information from which *historisch* props for faith can be built, but, on the contrary, because they confront us afresh with the scandal of faith which can have no such props. The scandal of the gospel is not that it contains no information that might help us believe in Jesus as the Christ, but that it contains information that might well lead us to disbelieve! Historical investigation finds nothing but the scandalous claim of this particular man that his words are the words of God, but what makes it scandalous is the apparent contradiction between the grandiose claim and the life of humility and rejection. Without the Gospel description of life and death the contradiction and therefore the full dimension of the scandal are not seen. A careful historical study of the Gospels, therefore, far from diminishing the scandal and eroding the basis for genuine faith, sets before us the decision of faith in its starkest terms: Can it be that this particular man, this Jew, son of a carpenter from an insignificant village, who gathered around him a small group of followers and was deserted by them as well as rejected and executed by the authorities, is what is claimed of him in the New Testament, the Christ of God?

"Was information about the manner of his historical life . . . necessary?"[63] asks Bultmann. The reply must be, "Yes," because only then is the reader confronted with the full implications of the decision of faith which affirms that, despite appearances, God is here revealed. God's revelation in Christ is hidden, not because there is nothing to be found, but because what *is* found does not look like God. Bultmann himself sees this point when he says approvingly of John's account of the life of Jesus that it "forms a unity framed by his coming and his departure [which] is both revelation and offense."[64] This offense is constituted precisely by what is known about the life of Jesus and is witnessed to not only in John but also in the Synoptics, and indeed throughout the New Testament.

7
MAN AND HIS EXISTENCE

WE HAVE SEEN how Bultmann's view of history has shaped his exegetical procedure, including the demythologizing project, and the way he uses this in reinterpreting the doctrines of revelation and Christology. In this concluding chapter the same influence will be seen at work in his understanding of man.

a. The centrality of the doctrine

Bultmann insists that the Bible must be read and interpreted in such a way that Biblical and theological affirmations are directly related to man's existence in the present. In a sense, therefore, the whole of Bultmann's theological enterprise can be seen as an all-inclusive doctrine of man. Man's existence is the topic for which reading the Bible is to provide material, and relevance for man's self-understanding is the norm to be used in testing the authenticity of doctrinal statements. This means, not that statements about God are to be eliminated in favor of statements about man, but that the one must always include the other. So the doctrine of man does not, in Bultmann's scheme, take the place of other doctrines, but other doctrines are seen at the same time to be aspects of the doctrine of man. For instance, in keeping with his view that "only such statements about God are legitimate as express the existentialist relation between God and man,"[1] Bultmann interprets the doctrine of creation primarily in terms of the creatureliness of man.[2] The same method is followed, as we have seen, in his discussion of revelation, incarnation, and salvation, where in each case they become aspects of the doctrine of man as he lives authentically or inauthentically, prior to or after the eschatological event. The outstanding illustration of the ubiquitous nature of the doctrine of man for Bultmann is, of course, his interpretation of Paul's theology, where he insists that "Paul's theology can best be treated as his doctrine of man: first, of man prior to the revelation of faith, and second, of man under faith."[3]

The extent to which this anthropological preoccupation is legitimate has already been discussed. The purpose of this recapitulation has been to show, before seeing how his view of history has influenced the *content* of Bultmann's doctrine of man, that this interpretation first establishes the *position* that it holds in his system. It is obvious enough that the centrality of this doctrine is due largely to Bultmann's conviction that history is something to be lived rather than observed. This means that the focal dimension is *Geschichtlichkeit*, so that the Bible as a historical document and Christianity as a historical religion must speak primarily to the existence of man in the present. It is therefore hardly surprising that all Biblical and theological affirmations can be seen as aspects of the doctrine of man.

b. Man as a historical being

Bultmann characteristically asserts that man is a historical rather than a natural being. What this implies becomes clearer as we recall the structure of history as Bultmann sees it, with the "history-nature" and *historisch-geschichtlich* distinctions, and the concepts of *Geschichtlichkeit* and *eschatologische Existenz.* First of all, this means that the real life of man is to be found in his relation to history rather than to nature, in the contingent encounters within history that demand decision and not in his relation to some timeless structure of Being. Therefore, man is what he is not because he has an essential nature that locates him within the eternal sphere of nature, but because God gives him his place according to his response to what he encounters in history. Insisting that this is, after all, the Biblical view, Bultmann says:

> The New Testament asserts that the real life of man is not that which appertains to the cosmos, but is to be found rather in what happens at any given time, in the sphere of the individual, and in the arena of history.[4]

> [Man] is not directed toward the general, the cosmos, in order to understand himself by seeking himself as a member of it . . . but he is rather directed toward his own concrete history.[5]

Therefore, to say that man is a historical being means, in the first place, that he is to be viewed in relation to history and its particular encounters rather than in relation to nature with its eternal structure. But this is not all it means, because since this is true of every man, this still deals with the individual only as one instance of the general classification "man." In other words, it still implies that man's nature (in this case a historical nature) is an instance of the nature of man in general.

Therefore, to say that man is historical means, in the second place, that each man has his own particular history, and it is this history which makes him what he is—this man and not an instance of man in general.[6] This history which each man has for himself (and which makes him who he is) is not merely the sum total of the things that have happened to him; it is what results according to the responses made to what has happened. To speak of man as a historical being is therefore to refer to his *Geschichtlichkeit*, his historicity, what he has become by virtue of his responsible decisions in encounter with *geschichtlich* events. This encounter is not to be thought of as a catalyst which somehow develops what is already latent within man; it is an event in which something new occurs, and in which man's existence is constituted. Therefore, Bultmann affirms, the real life of man comes to him out of the future and not out of the past, standing before him and acquiring its character as "forfeited or real by his decision."[7]

On one occasion Sartre was approached by a young man who, embittered by the horror and savagery of war, asked if there was any way of finding meaning in life. Sartre's reply was something like this: "Do as you like, as long as you do it wholeheartedly and with imagination. Invent the sort of self you are to be, and stick to your invention." Bultmann would agree with the last part of that. There is a real sense in which we make ourselves. Although our freedom is limited and many things happen to us that we did nothing to prompt and can do nothing to avoid, we are still free to respond to what happens, and in the context of these responses we make ourselves. "My real Self is always future possibility," says Bultmann. "It is realized ever anew in each successive decision."[8]

But while he might agree with the second part of Sartre's reply, Bultmann would question the first, claiming that it is important not only to invent a self but to invent the right kind of self. In other words, while it is necessary to begin a discussion of man by asserting that he is historical and therefore makes himself through his decisions, this by no means exhausts the content of the Christian doctrine of man, for this includes the kerygmatic affirmation of man as sinner who can be saved only by the act of God in Christ. How does Bultmann's view of history apply here?

c. *Inauthentic and authentic existence*

Bultmann's reinterpretation of the doctrine of man as sinner and saved relies heavily on the concepts of inauthentic and authentic existence as Heidegger elaborated them.[9] Inauthentic existence or the life of man prior to faith is characterized by man's being bound to the past, whereas authentic existence is open to the future. The transition from one to the other is achieved by the encounter with God's grace in the present. The full implications of this historicizing of the doctrine of man can be appreciated only when Heidegger's understanding of man's "being-in-the-world" is kept in mind because, as Macquarrie has shown, Bultmann makes extensive use of this idea.

For Heidegger, the defining characteristic of man is that he exists; but whereas in everyday language we use the term "existence" to describe minimal participation in life, often contrasting "merely existing" with "really living," Heidegger uses it in just the opposite way to point to the fullness of man's being in the world. *Existenz,* the mode of man's being, has the features of self-revelation (man is able to look at himself, and so is able to be subject and object at the same time), possibility (man does not have a fixed nature but becomes something new in each decision), and individuality (man is not just an instance of the class man; he is unique). This way of describing man's being in the world Bultmann uses in his exposition of Paul's use of the term *sōma.* This, Bultmann explains, cannot adequately be translated "body," for by it Paul is referring not to one aspect of man but to his whole mode of being in the world, the most significant feature of which is his self-relation, his being "able in a certain sense to distinguish himself from himself."[10]

But this is only part of the picture. Man's existence which has the features of self-relation, possibility, and individuality may be either inauthentic or authentic. In other words, since man's existence has the feature of possibility, he can choose how he will be related to himself and to others, and since he is constituted in decision, this will determine the form of his existence.

(i) *Inauthentic existence.* Because of his capacity for self-transcendence, man is able to view himself either as an individual and unique subject, or as an object among other objects in the world. Since the sense of individuality (which is part of the givenness of his existence) often threatens him with loneliness instead of liberating him, he becomes anxious and so seeks certainty and security within the world. Although man is an individual and his existence is his own, he tries to deny rather than to affirm this feature of his existence. He seeks to escape from loneliness and responsibility by identifying himself with the world, becoming engrossed in its concerns and merging himself with the crowd. This is the way that Heidegger describes inauthentic existence, pointing to the fallenness of man which is "the fundamental way of everyday living."[11]

It is clear once again that Bultmann uses these ideas in his exposition of Paul, saying:

> The characterization of man as *soma* implies, then, that man is a being who has a relationship to himself, and that this

relationship can be either an appropriate or a perverted one; that he can be at one with himself or at odds; that he can be under his own control or lose a grip on himself.[12]

He also extends this idea, showing that man's relation to the world, as to himself, may be authentic or inauthentic. In the authentic relation the world is the sphere of man's constructive activity; in the inauthentic relation it becomes the place where man loses himself. This distinction enables Bultmann to interpret the New Testament understanding of *kosmos* historically, referring primarily to man's attitude toward the world. This makes it possible for him to distinguish between two Pauline uses of the term, namely, *kosmos* as referring to "earthly conditions of life and earthly possibilities," and *kosmos* as constituting "the implicit or explicit antithesis to the sphere of God or 'the Lord.' "[13]

These characteristics of man's inauthentic or fallen existence Bultmann uses also in his interpretation of life without faith. For Bultmann as for Heidegger, the impetus that leads to fall is man's anxiety which he tries to overcome by turning toward the world as a source of security.[14] However, in this search man not only fails to find security but also loses his true life. He becomes captive to the very sphere in which he tries to find security. Therefore, the life of man without faith is a rejection of his true self in the search for security in the world. But it is more than this; according to Bultmann, it is at the same time "rebellion against God, who as Creator gave to man his being."[15] It is a turning away from the Creator toward the creation. It is living not only in flesh (a characteristic of every man's existence as man) but according to the flesh (a characteristic of every man's inauthentic or fallen existence).[16] The man who is afraid of losing what he has and so buries his one talent in the security of the earth not only fails to live his own life to the full but also rebels against God, who gave him the talent in the first place.

Having seen in broad outline how Heidegger's views of existence and fallenness have influenced Bultmann's interpretation of man as sinner, we can now relate this to the understanding of man as a historical being. For both Heidegger and Bultmann, as we have seen, to say that man is historical means more than that he exists "in time." It means that he constitutes his own historicity in the present by decision. But decision in relation to what? To both past and future, according to Heidegger, who sees past, present, and future as more than moments of time. They are aspects of man's temporality (*Zeitlichkeit*), which is "the original being of man."[17] Now, we have already seen that this existence of man is characterized by his being in the world (certain features of his existence are given to him), by his capacity for self-transcendence, and by his possibility. These three features of his existence can therefore be expressed as aspects of his temporality. First, the givenness of man's situation points to the dimension of the past; from the past come both the boundaries of the situation man finds himself in and what man has made of himself by his past decisions. Second, the capacity for self-relation refers to the present; man is able to stand off and take stock of himself here and now. Third, the possibility for man comes to him out of the future; this future stands before him, waiting to be chosen by his decision in the present. However, this balance between past, present, and future is upset because, as we have seen, man chooses to live inauthentically, looking upon himself as an object, his possibility as a threat, and the world as a place in which to hide. So he clings to the security of what the past has given him and made him, so that the past does not merely provide boundaries and the raw material of his life; it comes to determine his existence. Being bound to the past in this way, man is no longer open to the possibilities offered by the future.

It is this way of looking at the historicity of man which shapes Bultmann's view of the paradox of human existence in the world. As a historical being, man lives his life in relation to the encounters of history; but since he clings to the past, he does not allow present encounters to open the way to new self-understanding. So Bultmann says:

> This world of historical existence, which with its questions of decision constantly opens up the future of man, is the real

> world; yet at the same time it is unreal—it is an illusion and a pretence, because man shuts himself off from the future, on the basis of which he alone would live.[18]

Man can therefore find his authentic life only as he is able to rid himself of the past. This does not mean that the past is per se the realm of inauthentic existence; but man, by his decision, changes the primary role of the past from the neutral one of granting him his particular situation in the world to the tyrannical one of binding him to himself and the world, thus closing off the future. In this decision which is characteristic of inauthentic existence, man is alienated not only from himself and others (as in Heidegger) but also, according to Bultmann, from God, because this decision for the past is at the same time an assertion of self-reliance. It is an attitude of pride in what he has and what he has made of himself.[19] It is, in the final estimate, an unwillingness to lose himself.

(ii) *Authentic existence.* Bultmann sees the characteristics of inauthentic existence as the attempt to establish oneself in the world, self-alienation and alienation from God. The main features of authentic existence are, as might be expected, world renunciation (in a sense that will be examined later), a return to genuine self-understanding, and a return to God as the source of life. And just as a man lives inauthentically when he decides to understand himself in terms of the past, so he lives authentically when he decides to understand himself anew as open to the future.

At this point Bultmann indicates a depth to the fallenness of man that he says is missing in Heidegger's analysis. Genuine response to the call inviting him to recover his true selfhood is not a simple possibility for man.[20] To break free from past self-understanding is to make a new self, and man is incapable of doing that.[21] To be delivered from the bondage of the past is to be delivered from oneself, and this man cannot achieve by himself. It is something that can be given him only through God's act in Christ. So, in measuring the depth of man's fallenness Bultmann also shows the full extent of the Christian kerygma:

> As a result of his self-assertion, man is a totally fallen being. He is capable of knowing that his authentic life consists in self-commitment, but he is incapable of realizing it because however hard he tries he still remains what he is, self-assertive man. So in practice authentic life becomes possible only when man is delivered from himself. It is the claim of the New Testament that this is exactly what has happened. This is precisely the meaning of that which was wrought in Christ. At the very point where man can do nothing, God steps in and acts.[22]

The consequence of this act of God is that man's past to which he was bound is ended. He is set free for new decision. He is made open to the future. His sins are forgiven. "God has *acted* and the world—"this world"—has come to an end. *Man himself has been made new.*"[23]

This way of looking at God's achievement for man provides Bultmann with a way of interpreting into historical rather than metaphysical or juridical terms a number of theological concepts related to this event. So, for instance, the *grace of God* is now seen, not as a timeless quality of God or as a quasi-material entity that he distributes, but as the eschatological event itself which "takes effect for everyone who recognizes it as such."[24] Derivatively, God's grace is seen as "*the new situation* into which men of faith . . . are put."[25] The *forgiveness* of sin in this context is not to be looked upon in juridical terms as remission of punishment contingent upon some form of compensation made on our behalf.[26] It means simply:

> the obliteration of man's past, and taking him to be what he is not—the man of the future; it means relieving him of dread and thereby making him free for the future.[27]

Righteousness too is defined in relation to the eschatological event. It is not to be thought of as man's possession, a quality that he has in himself, but is simply descriptive of the new relationship that man has toward others and to God made possible by the eschatological event.[28] And, as we have already seen, in his reinterpretation of the *doctrine of the Spirit* in historical terms Bultmann turns away from the New Testament references to the Spirit as quasi-physical indwelling presence, insisting instead that Spirit is to be understood as a mode of man's being as genuinely historical, synonymous with eschatological existence. "The Spirit . . . is the possibility of new life which must be appropriated by a deliberate resolve."[29]

We have been looking at the way in which Bultmann's interpretation of man as inauthentic and authentic existence, and the transition between the two, is dependent upon his view of history and of man as historical. We have also seen, without going into any detail, that his view influences the understanding of a series of theological terms related to man's existence in the light of the eschatological event. This way of life opened to man by the eschatological event Bultmann calls "eschatological existence"; but he also insists that this life remains "historical" even when it is eschatological.[30] Man continues to live in the world even when the old world of his former self-understanding has passed away. What, then, are the characteristics of this life?

d. Life between the times

The traditional way of describing the life of the believer in the world is to say that he exists "between the times," between the past event of redemption and the inauguration or fulfillment of the Kingdom. Bultmann retains this terminology, but, as might be expected, effects a reinterpretation in which "between the times" is made to refer primarily to the character of human existence and not to its chronological framework.[31] In other words, the significance of "betweenness" is to be found within man's historicity. This reinterpretation follows directly from Bultmann's insistence that theological affirmations apply at the level of *Geschichtlichkeit* rather than *Weltgeschichte*. One implication of this is that the believer does not look back to an event in world history for his salvation but listens instead to a word which meets him in the present, speaking decisively to his situation. In the same way, he does not look toward a future event in world history as the fulfillment of God's act of redemption but finds instead in the present moment of decision that freedom for the future which is the continuing fulfillment of God's act of grace. This means that Bultmann cannot view the situation of the believer as one between the past act of redemption and the future coming of the Kingdom, since, for him, each of these concepts is significant only in the present existence of the believer. Therefore, Bultmann follows the same line of interpretation for "future Kingdom of God" that we saw him use for "past act of redemption":

> The future Kingdom of God . . . is not something which is to come in the course of time. . . . Rather the Kingdom of God is a power which, although it is entirely future, wholly determines the present. It determines the present because it now compels man to decision; he is determined thereby either in this direction or in that, as chosen or rejected, in his entire present existence.[32]

It is clear from this that Bultmann is using the term "future" not with the ordinary chronological connotation but, in the existentialist framework of meaning, as that which grants to man in the present the possibility of authentic decision. Thus the Kingdom of God is future not in the sense of coming later in the course of time but in the sense of granting to man the freedom to choose against his past self and for new self-understanding in relation to God.

Karl Löwith, to whom Bultmann acknowledges indebtedness for discussions on the philosophy-theology relation,[33] criticizes the above interpretation. He says that by pointing to the instant of our decision as the locus for the true futurity of the *eschaton*, Bultmann

> ignores the fact that neither death nor the Kingdom of God could ever provoke a decision, and even less a radical change in man's conduct and attitude, unless they were expected as real events in the future.[34]

By "real event in the future" Löwith obviously means an event in future world history, and Bultmann would certainly deny this. Just as a past event in world history means nothing to man until it is made a present event in personal history, so a future event in world history can mean nothing until it becomes part of present personal history. However, Löwith's criticism does point to an incongruity in the way Bultmann deals with past and future events, for whereas Bultmann affirms that there was an indispensable occurrence in the past which, through preaching, becomes of decisive importance for the present, he makes no equivalent affirmation about a world-historical event in the future. For some reason that he certainly does not explain, Bultmann holds that the kerygma would be destroyed if reference to God's past act in Christ were removed, but not when reference to the future fulfillment is eliminated.

For Bultmann, then, the "no longer" and the "not yet" of the believer's life in the world refer to the character of his existence and not to its location in world history between past and future happening. What, then, are the features of this existence? There are two major ones, closely related yet distinguishable. The first is that man's life is lived under the imperative based on an indicative; the second, that he lives withdrawn from yet responsible for the world.

(i) The "no longer" aspect of man's existence refers to the fact that he is no longer bound to his past understanding of himself. The old world of his old self is no longer operative. The world in the sense of that which holds man in bondage and in separation from God has lost its power. But man is "not yet" free from the givenness of his earthly life. He still lives in the world. The world in the sense of the context in which man lives is still operative. Therefore, while man is now free for genuine decision and authentic action, these must still be in accord with God's will which is made known nowhere else but in man's situation in the world. Bultmann generally puts the point this way: Whereas before the eschatological event the imperative to do God's will condemned man because he was not free to choose obedience, now man is free from the past and is no longer condemned by the imperative because he can now obey. Because of the indicative—that man is given his freedom—the imperative is now a genuine possibility as well as a continuing requirement. So Bultmann says of the life of faith: "As a new life no longer belonging to the old æon it can be described in the indicative; but as long as it must be led in the old world, it stands under the imperative."[35] This, of course, is the basis for a genuinely Christian ethic which sees obedience not as a prerequisite for receiving God's grace but as a response made possible by the eschatological event.

(ii) The event that places the believer in eschatological existence is also described by Bultmann as taking him away from the world.[36] But this is not seen as asceticism or escapism. What is being renounced is not the world in the sense of the context for man's life but in the sense of that within which man finds security and to which he has consequently bound himself by his own decision to live inauthentically. Therefore, withdrawal from the world which is a feature of authentic existence means a reversal of the decision for the creation rather than the Creator. It means a break with the past self-understanding in which man decided to merge with the crowd, losing his identity in the world. It means restoration of the possibility of free decision by which one's historicity may be renewed. These phrases sound familiar because this is just the way Bultmann talks about freedom from the past, and in fact he explicitly acknowledges the correlation between "withdrawal from the world" and "freedom from the past" when he says:

> The believer is "taken out of the world" in that he does not think that he has the truth in any knowledge which he possesses, but, forgetting what lies behind him, continually reaches out to what lies ahead of him.[37]

It is clear from this that Bultmann thinks of withdrawal from the world in existential-historical rather than cosmological or metaphysical terms. Man is not being absolved from responsibility in the world. On the contrary, he is set free for decision in which he is responsible directly to God, who encounters him in the world.

It is this understanding of withdrawal from the world which provides the basis for Bultmann's characteristic reference to the Christian ethic as one of radical obedience. Being withdrawn from the world (which is equivalent to being free from the past) means being free from having to accept the world's estimate of right and wrong. It means being free from formal authority and from the binding power of ethical theories that lay down rules for action prior to the event. It means being free from the obligation of acting in the present upon the precedent of the past.[38] It means being free for a decision in which man stands in the present before the demand of God and in which his whole being is at stake. Therefore, eschatological existence is at the same time ethical, for in the continuing call to radical obedience before God lies the possibility of new being:

> Renunciation of the world represents no escapism or asceticism, but an otherworldliness which is simply being ready for God's command, summoning men to abandon all earthly ties. On the positive side and complementary to it is the commandment of love, in which a man turns away from self and places himself at the disposal of others. In so doing, he has decided for God.[39]

In his study of Bultmann's ethics,[40] Thomas Oden shows very clearly how the theme of radical obedience dominates, and that it owes its dominant place to Bultmann's emphasis on the historicity of man. This, however, becomes the point at which Oden criticizes Bultmann most severely. Directing attention to the Now of eschatological decision "anthropologizes the relation between God and man,"[41] according to Oden, so that the radical obedience becomes merely an attitude of the self in the moment. This means that while man may feel a demand in the moment, the Lord who calls man to obedience is excluded and the demand is emptied of content because continuity with the past is nullified.

However, this criticism of Oden overlooks one vital point, namely, that for Bultmann self-understanding arises in the confrontation with one who is other, and this confrontation takes place not in some kind of mystical experience, not when one is somehow removed from the demands of the world but precisely when, in particular situations in the world, one has to decide between different courses of action. Far from excluding the Lord from such moments of call to radical obedience, Bultmann affirms that it is in just such moments that the Lord comes to meet us. As he says in his response to Oden, "In the moment one meets the *transcendent* divine demand in the attire of *concrete* obligation."[42]

With the other point of Oden's criticism concerning a lack of continuity with the past and a consequent lack of content to the demand I have more sympathy. In particular, I think Bultmann could give far greater place than he does to the relevance of Jesus' teaching for obedient response in the present. This is not to say that we should somehow bypass the other New Testament proclamation and try to get back to some more authentic basis for Christian ethic, but, following a point made earlier, that we should accept the Synoptic Gospels as being the proclamation of the church designed as Paul and John are (although using different literary techniques) to elicit response and not just to pass on facts. Since Bultmann uses some of the Pauline and Johannine material to indicate not the particular decisions that we ought to come to but how we ought to approach contemporary decisions so that radical obedience is possible, so the Synoptic accounts of the life and teaching of Jesus can be used in the same way. Such an approach is not excluded either by Bultmann's existentialist orientation or by his demythologizing project. In fact, as Heinz Horst Schrey has suggested,[43] this project might well be extended directly into the realm of Christian ethics. Just as the presuppositions of thought have changed since New Testament times, demanding a transposition of the kerygma into contemporary thought patterns, so the ideas and structures of society have changed, demanding a similar transposition of attitudes toward society and the self:

> If a theological ethic tries to uphold ancient social norms under different conditions of life, it tends to become an ideology. . . . Therefore, in ethics there is a parallel task to demythologizing which may be termed deideologizing.[44]

According to Schrey, Bultmann has agreed that such a project would be in harmony with his own.

e. The church, historical and eschatological

In one final area of Bultmann's thought the dominant influence of his view of history can be seen, namely, in his understanding of the church. This has received very little attention, partly because Bultmann has not written very much at all that could be classified as a doctrine of the church, and partly because it is generally assumed that to concentrate so much on personal historicity is to leave little room for the community of faith. However, a great deal of what Bultmann has written has direct relevance for the doctrine of the church, and it is by no means true that the theme has no interest for Bultmann and is excluded by his existentialist approach. Hans Bolewski[45] has written a persuasive article on the role of the church in Bultmann's theology in which he argues that the question of what the church is and how it is related to the other phenomena of history has been a dominating feature of Bultmann's thought from the beginning, and that his conclusions provide significant guidelines for contemporary discussion of this theme. To work out these implications would be a worthwhile undertaking, but beyond the scope of this work. It remains for us simply to see how Bultmann's view of history is operative here.

The best place to start is with Bultmann's own description of the church as the eschatological community. This is hardly an original description. Those who come to faith participate in the community of faith; or, to use Bultmann's terminology, those who are reconstituted in the light of the eschatological event are part of the community of those who are living an eschatological existence. But what is the relationship between the eschatological community and the visible organization or institution in the world that we call the church? The relationship, Bultmann holds, is a paradoxical one; but this does not mean that nothing more can be said. In describing the relationship, Bultmann uses the familiar terms "visible" and "invisible." Since the church is a fellowship of the Spirit, he says:

> It is essentially invisible to the world. In one sense, of course, it is visible, like the Gnostic communities. It consists of real

> men and women, who still live "in the flesh." But here we are faced with a paradox. This conglomeration of believers is also the eschatological community, the "body of Christ," whose existence is not subject to objective proof.[46]

There is an obvious parallel here between Bultmann's view of the "visible institution"–"eschatological community" relation and his understanding of the "Jesus of history"–"eschatological event" relation. In both cases the paradox can be described in the same way, viz., that a *historisch* person or institution is at the same time eschatological. In the historical life of Jesus and of the church God is acting, but in neither case can the *historisch* approach establish that he is there at work. Here an echo from Luther is clearly heard, for he too understood the hiddenness of God as applying both to Jesus and to the life of the church. According to Luther, no one knew what God was doing in the humble birth, the self-giving life, the scandalous death of Jesus; neither was "that puny band," the disciples, recognized as the sphere of God's action; nor does the world see now what God is doing through his weak, divided, and sinful church. "The eye cannot discern," Luther was fond of saying; "only the ear can hear." Bultmann agrees. Jesus of Nazareth becomes the saving event as he is proclaimed and heard in the Word; the church is eschatological community as its life and word become the Word now addressing man. Just as there is no way of verifying that Jesus Christ is the eschatological event apart from the event in which he is proclaimed and responded to, so there is no way of verifying that the visible institution is the eschatological community apart from the event in which the Word addresses men through the life and words of the church. Therefore, the church cannot guarantee faith because it is itself an object of faith; it is "just as much a scandal as the cross."[47]

The church, then, is eschatological community because it is called into being by the Word that addresses men and opens the way to eschatological existence, and remains eschatological as the Word is still proclaimed through its life and words. But this does not mean that the church can have no order or structure, no institutional form, no continuing history. Every human society must depend for its continuing existence in history upon regulations and order, and this is not alien to the church as eschatological community because, as we have seen, the paradox of the church is that it is at the same time a "conglomeration of believers" and the body of Christ, a human society and the eschatological community. The question facing the church, therefore, is not how to be the eschatological community by doing away with all institutional forms but how to develop institutional forms that enable it to retain and express its eschatological self-understanding. Bultmann does not answer this question directly but, characteristically, expresses his view through his exegesis of Paul and John. Part IV of his *Theology of the New Testament* on the "Development Toward the Ancient Church" is largely preoccupied with that question, and in the course of the discussion Bultmann makes it clear that the gradual institutionalizing of the church did result in a loss of eschatological awareness, although this need not have occurred.

But what does Bultmann mean by "eschatological awareness"? The awareness of living between the times, naturally enough. However—and this is the clue to what is distinctive about Bultmann's view of the church—"between the times" is interpreted existentially rather than chronologically. For Bultmann, the individual lives "between the times" in the sense that his present existence is open to the future, not bound to the past; the reference is to a feature of man's historicity rather than to his being located between two events in world history, one past and one present. In the same way, in his understanding of the church's life between the times Bultmann says that this refers primarily to its being called by God to proclaim in the present the saving event of Christ which now sets men free. But the ironical fact is that this genuine proclamation of the eschatological "now" of salvation is lost when the church begins to couch its proclamation in what have become the traditional eschatological terms. When eschatological existence is proclaimed as future possibility rather than as present reality, the present life of the believer is no longer seen as eschatological existence in the here-and-now but as "the condition for achieving future salvation."[48] This loss of the genuinely eschatological dimension in its proclamation is accompanied by a loss of the church's own self-understanding as an eschatological community. It no longer sees itself as the community of those who know the new life, the community which manifests the new æon in its own life, but as an institution which will enable its members to participate in the future *eschaton*. Because, as Bultmann puts it, "the 'betweenness' of the present is conceived as that which determines only the chronology of the Christian situation and not its character,"[49] both the church's proclamation and its life lose their genuinely eschatological character. "The church has changed from a fellowship of salvation to an institution of salvation."[50]

There are, of course, difficulties in Bultmann's view, some of which are cited by Bolewski. It may, for instance, be difficult to sustain as sharply as Bultmann suggests the contrast between the Pauline and Deutero-Pauline views of the church. Käsemann may be right when he argues that the authority of the institutional ministry was not a degeneration from the Pauline view of the church but was made necessary by the excessive demands Paul made on individuals and a loosely organized fellowship.[51] My main criticism is that at several points Bultmann has apparently ignored his own interpretation of what it means to see the church as eschatological community. His insistence, for instance, that the church is "genuine Church only as an event which happens each time here and now"[52] leads to a punctiliar view of the church, tearing apart the church as historical entity and eschatological community and so destroying the paradox that Bultmann has elsewhere been so careful to preserve. This paradox is also overlooked when Bultmann asserts that "those who are united in the Church are not bound together by any worldly interests or motives."[53] This is demonstrably untrue of the church as a visible community in the world. Those who are part of that community are united for many different and often worldly interests. Bultmann's own view of the church should allow him to acknowledge that fact, while affirming at the same time that this "conglomeration of believers" is also united by the eschatological deed of God manifest in Christ.

Despite these criticisms and the fact that Bultmann has given little attention to working out a detailed ecclesiology, I agree with Bolewski that in his writings Bultmann provides a number of insights which can give valuable direction to the current discussions. In particular, Bultmann's views allow us to ask the central question about the shape and direction the church should now take in the mid-twentieth century without having the answer determined by past forms of the institutional church, by patterns of ministry discernible in the early church, or by principles of continuity between the old and the new Israel. The central question is: What form of life will now enable the church to proclaim through life and word the eschatological act of God? Attention to the past may inform, but will not determine, the answer.

8
CONCLUSION

THE PURPOSE OF THIS BOOK has been to show how Bultmann's view of history has influenced both his theological method and his doctrinal formulations. During the course of the discussion a number of conclusions were drawn and criticisms made, and there is little point in recapitulating them here. However, some comments should be made about the force of these criticisms. Are they peripheral, or do they threaten the whole structure? Can they be corrected from within, or do we need to go outside the system and begin all over again?

I have argued that the most persistent and damaging criticism of Bultmann, namely, that his continuing stress on the act of God in Jesus Christ is fundamentally at odds with his whole project, cannot be sustained. If my argument is accepted, this removes one of the main threats to the system as a whole. However, an equally fundamental question began to emerge during the discussion of Bultmann's hermeneutical method. It became clear that large areas of the New Testament are excluded from exegetical attention by Bultmann's approach. Bultmann claims that since these areas are impervious to his hermeneutical principle of approaching the New Testament with the question of human existence, they represent either a deviation from the genuine kerygma or, at best, a very minor theme. In either case they may be ignored. But it could be argued with equal logical force that since these areas do not respond to Bultmann's approach, the fault lies with the approach and not with the excluded areas. Those who take this latter view might then reject Bultmann's approach *in toto*, claiming that while it may elucidate some aspects of the New Testament its failure to throw light on the rest shows that the whole project was misconceived. This in turn calls into question Bultmann's view of history which provides the framework for the whole endeavor.

My own preference is to find a way between these alternatives. I am basically in agreement with Bultmann's view of history and with the hermeneutical principles that result, although I cannot accept his occasional use of these principles as a device for excluding from consideration those passages and doctrines which do not appear to conform. However, I do not think it is necessary to jettison the whole project because of this aberration. In the first place, a more careful application of Bultmann's own historicocritical methods shows that some areas of the New Testament are more concerned with the question of human existence than he acknowledges. He seems strangely reluctant, for instance, to draw out the implications of his own conclusion that the Synoptic Gospels as well as Paul and John are concerned to proclaim Jesus in the light of kerygmatic Christology rather than to give an objective-historical outline of his life. If Bultmann had taken this seriously, his *Theology of the New Testament* would have included far more attention to the proclamation of the Christ event through the Synoptics and would consequently have been a better balanced work. In the second place, it should be admitted that in some parts of the New Testament the authors' concern for the question of human existence does seem to be a secondary one. But this does not mean either that these should be excluded or that Bultmann's approach should be abandoned. If the most basic of his hermeneutical principles is applied, viz., that the interpreter should bring to the text the question that concerned the author, this would mean admitting that the question of human existence appropriate in most cases is not appropriate in others, and that the history which interests some of the writers is not the historicity of man but, for instance, the history of the nation. It would also open the way to finding another series of questions that would elucidate these passages. Such an approach is not, I think, fundamentally out of harmony with Bultmann's project;

it recognizes the diversity of New Testament witness and allows the Word to address man through this diversity.

As far as Bultmann's doctrinal formulations are concerned, I have shown how his view of history has influenced his understanding of the revelation of God, God's act in Christ, and the existence of man. I believe that in these areas Bultmann's conclusions are on the whole consistent with his view of history and theological method. This was argued at some length, particularly in relation to Bultmann's stress on Christ as the act of God in history, where it was shown that as long as Bultmann's view of history and of historical event is accepted, then it is not inconsistent with his demythologizing principles to speak of God's act in Christ as a historical event. However, there is no doubt that at many points of doctrine Bultmann's views, while internally consistent, are at variance with traditional interpretation. For example, according to Bultmann, the history of Israel is not history of revelation for the Christian; Jesus is not the Christ event in world history but becomes such in the proclamation and hearing of the Word; the *extra nos* feature of God's act is retained only in a special sense; the resurrection of Christ is not an event in history following the crucifixion but is the dimension of meaning of the cross; and so on.

As before, there are two ways of reacting to this break with traditional understanding. One may accept Bultmann's view of history and hermeneutics, and therefore his doctrinal conclusions which do meet the conditions of validity that he has set down. Or one may argue from the opposite direction, claiming that the norm for valid theological conclusions is coherence with traditional doctrinal patterns. Then Bultmann's interpretations and the structure of history on which they are based will be rejected. Once again I prefer to find a way between these alternatives, introducing modifications to Bultmann's views while not abandoning his basic approach. Such a way was suggested in the discussion that began with Gogarten's emphasis on Jesus' obedient proclamation of the word. This makes it possible to introduce significant modifications to Bultmann's thought (e.g., that the act of God in Christ originates in the life of

Jesus and his obedience to the message of salvation, so that he is Messiah prior to the preaching of the early church) while still remaining within the context of Bultmann's theological method.

The last word has yet to be written about Bultmann. My purpose has been to show that whatever the last word may be, the first word ought to be *history*.

NOTES

ABBREVIATIONS

E & F	*Existence and Faith: Shorter Writings of Rudolf Bultmann*
Essays	*Essays: Philosophical and Theological*
G. *und* V.	*Glauben und Verstehen*, 3 vols.
H & E	*History and Eschatology*
JC & M	*Jesus Christ and Mythology*
K & M	*Kerygma and Myth: A Theological Debate*
ThNT	*Theology of the New Testament*, 2 vols.

1. INTRODUCTION: AN EXISTENTIALIST APPROACH

1. Carl Michalson, ed., *Christianity and the Existentialists* (Charles Scribner's Sons, 1956), p. 2.

2. Friedrich Gogarten, *Demythologizing and History*, tr. by N. H. Smith (London: SCM Press, Ltd., 1955), p. 28. Bultmann, of course, acknowledges his dependence upon Dilthey, but he also indicates that this approach was already present in the historical relativists. They too emphasized the immersion of man within the stream of history, although they mistakenly interpreted this as total determination (Rudolf Bultmann, *History and Eschatology* [Edinburgh: Edinburgh University Press, 1957], p. 143). Gogarten goes farther, claiming that this approach to history stems from the Scriptures and was found again in Luther, in contrast to the metaphysical tradition of dogma that generally espoused views oriented toward Hellenism.

3. *H & E*, p. 143.

4. *Ibid.*, p. 117.

5. *Ibid.*, p. 127.

6. Rudolf Bultmann, "Meaning in History," *Listener*, September, 1955, p. 329.

7. *Ibid.*

8. R. G. Collingwood, *The Idea of History* (Oxford University Press, 1956), p. 215.

9. I.e., "realized in the active sense of "made real"; see the above quotation from Bultmann (n.7) in which he says of meaning in history that we realize it in responsible decisions.

10. These are the questions that appear again and again when Bultmann's views are being considered. Many of them appear in rhetorical form, the implication being that the answer is obvious, e.g., Barth's ironical approach to the attempt to understand Bultmann (*Kerygma und Mythos*, ed. by Hans Werner Bartsch, 2 vols. [Hamburg: Herbert Reich-Evangelischer Verlag, 1948], Vol. II, pp. 86 ff.). However, when the questions are put in this rhetorical-critical way they often betray a gross misunderstanding of Bultmann's view of history and consequently of the approach to exegesis and doctrine that presupposes this view.

2. The Structure of History

1. Rudolf Bultmann, *Jesus* (Tübingen: J. C. B. Mohr, Paul Siebeck, 1951); English translation, *Jesus and the Word*, by L. P. Smith and E. H. Lantero (Charles Scribner's Sons, 1934 and 1958); quotation from the 1958 edition, p. 3.

2. In his reply to Paul Minear, in *The Theology of Rudolf Bultmann*, ed. by Charles W. Kegley (London: SCM Press, Ltd., 1966), pp. 266–267.

3. *Primitive Christianity in Its Contemporary Setting*, tr. by R. H. Fuller (Living Age Book, Meridian Books, Inc., 1956), pp. 103–104.

4. *Ibid.*, p. 20.

5. Heinrich Ott, *Geschichte und Heilsgeschichte in der Theologie Rudolf Bultmanns* (Tübingen: J. C. B. Mohr, 1955), p. 10.

6. In Kegley, ed., *op. cit.*, p. 267.

7. This charge is seen in various forms in the essays in *Kerygma und Mythos*. Thielicke, Schniewind, and Barth all make this criticism. Despite Bultmann's insistence that he does not intend at all to ignore the connection between faith on the one hand and the

cross of Christ on the other, and that his concern is with the present significance of the indubitably essential past-historical event, critics writing later press just the same charges. See especially the essays by Künneth and Kinder in *The Historical Jesus and the Kerygmatic Christ,* ed. and tr. by Carl E. Braaten and Roy A. Harrisville (Abingdon Press, 1964).

8. Especially Schubert Ogden, who returns again and again to the complaint first made in his doctoral dissertation that Bultmann cannot retain his emphasis on God's unique act in Christ while being consistent with the principles outlined in the demythologizing project.

9. His own work in *Jesus* employs this method.

10. Bultmann's most careful explanation of the meaning of the statement "God acts in history" is found in *Jesus Christ and Mythology* (Charles Scribner's Sons, 1958), pp. 60–85.

11. *Essays: Philosophical and Theological,* English translation of *Glauben und Verstehen,* by James C. G. Greig (The Macmillan Company, 1955), p. 72.

12. *Essays,* pp. 124–125.

13. So, e.g., in his interpretation of the doctrine of man (*Essays,* pp. 67–89) he shows that a Biblical understanding demands concentrating in the dimension of present decision and encounter. And he sees the doctrine of creation (*Existence and Faith: Shorter Writings of Rudolf Bultmann,* tr. by Schubert M. Ogden [Living Age Book, Meridian Books, Inc., 1960], pp. 171–183), answering questions about the historicity of man rather than the origin of the natural world.

14. *Kerygma and Myth: A Theological Debate,* ed. by Hans Werner Bartsch, tr. from Vol. I of *Kerygma und Mythos* (Harper Torchbook, Harper & Brothers, 1961), p. 82.

15. For instance, he sometimes uses the adjective *geschichtlich* simply to indicate that an event actually happened in the past, although he usually employs *historisch* for that purpose. And although he criticizes Barth for using the term *Geschichte* to refer to a complex of happenings instead of the present history in which I stand, he sometimes does this himself.

16. *JC & M,* p. 80.

17. *Theology of the New Testament,* tr. by Kendrick Grobel (Charles Scribner's Sons, 1954) Vol. II, p. 69. Used by permission.

18. Bultmann's reply, in Kegley, ed., *op. cit.,* p. 267.

19. *G. und* V., Vol. I, p. 317.

20. *Primitive Christianity*, p. 3.

21. In Kegley, ed., *op. cit.*, p. 267.

22. To use, in a different way, a well-known illustration from H. Richard Niebuhr.

23. *Kerygma und Mythos*, Vol. I, p. 47.

24. In Kegley, ed., *op. cit.*, p. 275.

25. *Ibid.*, p. 274.

26. Ott, *op. cit.*, p. 4.

27. Within this dimension Bultmann sees "history considered as the affairs of nations" (*ThNT*, Vol. I, p. 25), or the history of a people "viewed as a real, empirical, historical entity" (*Essays*, p. 192). Within this realm is to be found Jesus of Nazareth insofar as he is "an objectifiable historical phenomenon" (*ibid.*, p. 288). Any *historisch* investigation that seeks to find out what actually happened can establish facts that inhere only within this dimension of *Weltgeschichte*, "world history."

28. *Listener*, September, 1955, p. 329.

29. *H & E*, p. 141.

30. *Ibid.*, p. 136.

31. *Ibid.*

32. Gogarten, *op. cit.*, p. 19.

33. *H & E*, p. 150.

34. *Essays*, p. 289.

35. *Ibid.*, p. 207.

36. *K & M*, p. 107.

37. Rudolf Bultmann, "History and Eschatology in the New Testament," *New Testament Studies*, Vol. 1 (September, 1954), p. 14.

38. J. S. Bezzant, "Demythologizing the Gospel," *Theology*, Vol. 57, No. 408 (June, 1954), p. 212.

39. *Essays*, pp. 182–208. Cited by John McIntyre, *The Christian Doctrine of History* (Edinburgh: Oliver & Boyd, Ltd., 1957), p. 66, who sees the variation but not the theme.

40. *JC & M*, p. 12.

41. *Listener*, September, 1955, p. 330.

42. *Essays*, pp. 286–287.

43. *Ibid.*, p. 85.

44. *Essays*, p. 110; cf. p. 289; *K & M*, pp. 20–21; *ThNT*, Vol. I, p. 19; Vol. II, *passim*.

45. *K & M*, p. 20.
46. In Kegley, ed., *op. cit.*, p. 280.
47. *JC & M*, p. 53.
48. *H & E*, p. 155.
49. *Essays*, p. 260.

3. The Problem of Hermeneutics

1. *ThNT*, Vol. II, p. 251.
2. Rudolf Bultmann, "Das Problem einer theologischen Exegese des Neuen Testaments," *Zwischen den Zeiten*, Vol. III (1925), pp. 334–357.
3. Bultmann's growing concern for theological method is reflected in the topics of his major works. *Die Geschichte der synoptischen Tradition* (1921) and *Jesus* (1926) were among his earlier works and employ an approach that he would now claim to be necessary but preliminary. The results from this kind of work were used in his commentary on John (1941). In the same year his essay on demythologizing appeared, calling for a method of interpretation that would use all the scholarly techniques, at the same time confronting the man of today with a message relevant to his own existence. His *Theologie des Neuen Testaments* (1948, 1951, 1953) is the result of applying such a method.
4. *Essays*, p. 235.
5. E.g., Helmut Thielicke, "Reflections on Bultmann's Hermeneutic," *Expository Times*, Vol. LXVII (1956), pp. 154 ff.; Karl Barth, "Rudolf Bultmann—An Attempt to Understand Him," *Kerygma und Mythos*, Vol. II, pp. 83 ff.
6. Gustav Wingren, *Theology in Conflict* (Muhlenberg Press, 1948), p. xiii.
7. *Essays*, p. 261.
8. *Ibid.*
9. *E & F*, pp. 289 ff.
10. *Essays*, p. 243.
11. *Ibid.*, p. 247.
12. *Ibid.*
13. *Ibid.*, p. 254.
14. *E & F*, p. 289.
15. *JC & M*, p. 53.
16. *ThNT*, Vol. II, p. 251.

17. *Essays*, p. 257.
18. John Macquarrie, *An Existentialist Theology* (London: SCM Press, Ltd., 1955).
19. Gogarten, *op. cit.*, pp. 57–58.
20. This charge is made by a number of critics, e.g., H. Thielicke, *K & M*, p. 150; Ian Henderson, *Myth in the New Testament* (Alec R. Allenson, Inc., 1952), pp. 30 f.; K. Barth, *Kerygma und Mythos*, Vol. II, pp. 83 ff.; Karl Jaspers and Rudolf Bultmann, *Myth and Christianity: An Inquiry Into the Possibility of Religion Without Myth* (The Noonday Press, 1958), pp. 8–9.
21. *JC & M*, p. 48.
22. Barth, *Kerygma und Mythos*, Vol. II, p. 121.
23. *Essays*, p. 136.
24. *JC & M*, p. 55.
25. Schumann, *K & M*, p. 186.
26. Bultmann, *JC & M*, pp. 57–58.
27. *ThNT*, Vol. II, p. 251.
28. *Ibid.*, p. 180.
29. *Ibid.*, p. 186.
30. Rudolf Bultmann, "History and Eschatology in the New Testament," *loc. cit.*, p. 12.
31. *ThNT*, Vol. I, p. 191.
32. *Ibid.*, Vol. II, p. 15.
33. *Ibid.*, p. 38.
34. *H & E*, p. 151.
35. *Ibid.*; cf. pp. 33, 42.
36. *ThNT*, Vol. I, p. 335.
37. *Ibid.*, p. 333.
38. *Ibid.*, p. 334.
39. *Ibid.*
40. *K & M*, pp. 21–22.
41. *H & E*, p. 42.
42. *ThNT*, Vol. II, p. 149.

4. The Demythologizing Project

1. Wingren, *op. cit.*, p. 133. Wingren actually makes this comment for the wrong reason, as he fails to see the difference between Bultmann's project and previous attempts made by others.
2. English translation, *Jesus and the Word*.

3. *Ibid.*, p. 11.

4. Bultmann himself locates the project within the intention of his work as a whole, insisting that "its aim is not to eliminate the mythological statements but to interpret them. It is a method of hermeneutics" (*JC & M*, p. 18).

5. *K & M*, p. 10, n. 2.

6. *JC & M*, p. 15.

7. Jaspers and Bultmann, *Myth and Christianity*, pp. 6–7.

8. *Ibid.*

9. *K & M*, p. 3.

10. *JC & M*, p. 19; cf. *Kerygma und Mythos*, Vol. II, p. 184.

11. *JC & M*, p. 40.

12. *K & M*, pp. 52, 84.

13. Jaspers and Bultmann, *Myth and Christianity*, p. 59.

14. E.g., in his *Die Christliche Hoffnung und das Problem der Entmythologisierung* (Stuttgart: Evangelisches Verlagswerk, 1954), pp. 21 f., Bultmann does imply that since the conception of hope dominant in the New Testament is compounded of Jewish apocalyptic and Gnostic ideas, it should, for just this reason, be demythologized.

15. *K & M*, p. 3.

16. *JC & M*, p. 80.

17. E.g., *K & M*, pp. 191–192.

18. This insistence arises, as we have seen, from Bultmann's view of history, in which he claims that the purpose of studying history is to "realize consciously the possibilities it affords for the understanding of human existence" (*ibid.*, p. 192), and that since the New Testament is a historical document, it must be approached in this way.

19. *Ibid.*, p. 13.

20. *Ibid.*, p. 15.

21. John Macquarrie's *The Scope of Demythologizing* (London: SCM Press, Ltd., 1960) takes as its point of departure this cross fire of criticism that comes from different directions but converges at the question of Bultmann's consistency.

22. Karl Barth, *Rudolf Bultmann, ein Versuch ihn zu Verstehen* (Zollikon-Zurich: Evangelischer Verlag, 1952), p. 6.

23. *ThNT*, Vol. I, p. 191.

24. *Glauben und Verstehen*, 3 vols. (Tübingen: J. C. B. Mohr, 1952), Vol. I, pp. 36–37.

25. Ogden argues that this is the basic feature of Bultmann's theology, "providing the necessary perspective from which to view all his writing" (*E & F*, p. 14).

26. E.g., *Jesus and the Word*, p. 151; *Essays*, pp. 11–12, 280–281; *Primitive Christianity*, p. 18; *JC & M*, p. 69.

27. Karl Barth, *Die kirchliche Dogmatik* (Zollikon-Zurich: Evangelischer Verlag A.G., 1948), III/2, p. 534; cited by Bultmann, *Essays*, p. 259.

28. W. Künneth, in *Ein Wort Lutheranischer Theologie zur Entmythologisierung*, ed. by E. Kinder (Munich: Evangelischer Pressverband, 1952), p. 78.

29. G. Beasley-Murray, *Listener*, September, 1955, p. 601.

30. H. Thielicke, *K & M*, pp. 146–147; cf. Macquarrie, *An Existentialist Theology*, pp. 242–243.

31. Thielicke, *K & M*, p. 146.

32. *K & M*, p. 203.

33. Macquarrie, *An Existentialist Theology*, p. 54. This reply is appropriate also to J. H. Thomas, who, in an article in the *Scottish Journal of Theology*, Vol. 10 (1957), makes much of what he calls the "obvious general point, that Bultmann's orientation is toward a philosophy of existence." Yet, in criticizing him for translating the gospel into terms of self-understanding, he completely neglects the existential depth of *Selbstverständnis*, projecting on Bultmann an alien intellectualist view of understanding.

34. I. Henderson, *op. cit.*, p. 29; cf. Macquarrie, *An Existentialist Theology*, p. 66.

35. Barth, *Die kirchliche Dogmatik*, III/2, p. 534.

36. For Bultmann's argument that since man is historical, faith as self-understanding is not a subjective event but arises in encounter with others, see *JC & M*, pp. 70–71.

37. *Essays*, pp. 259–260; cf. *ThNT*, Vol. II, p. 239; *JC & M*, pp. 75–76.

5. The Revelation of God in History

1. Oscar Cullmann, in his *Christ and Time* (The Westminster Press, 1950), sees this in relation to the time line of history and locates Christ at the midpoint.

2. R. Bultmann, "Heilsgeschichte und Geschichte," *Theologische Literaturzeitung*, November, 1948, pp. 659–666.

3. *ThNT*, Vol. II, p. 116.
4. E.g., Heb., ch. 1, Acts, chs. 6–7.
5. *ThNT*, Vol. II, p. 117.
6. Cullmann, *op. cit.*, p. 20.
7. *ThNT*, Vol. I, p. 319.
8. As espoused, for instance, by Will Herberg in his article "Biblical Faith as *Heilsgeschichte*," *Christian Scholar*, Vol. 39 (March, 1956), pp. 25 ff. There he insists that "redemptive history is not merely a recital . . . [it] is also a demand upon us" (p. 31).
9. Except in the sense that historical involvement with the past is always a possibility. But in this sense, Bultmann holds, any past is equally significant for "Occidental history" and equally irrelevant for our personal history as Christians.
10. *G. und V.*, Vol. I, p. 333.
11. *Essays*, p. 191.
12. Bultmann, "History and Eschatology in the New Testament," *loc. cit.*, p. 13.
13. G. E. Wright, *God Who Acts* (London: SCM Press, Ltd., 1952), made this view popular.
14. *H & E*, p. 16.
15. *Ibid.*, p. 13.
16. *G. und V.*, Vol. I, p. 332.
17. *Ibid.*, pp. 332–333.
18. *Ibid.*, p. 333.
19. *Ibid.*, p. 325.
20. *Ibid.*, p. 317.
21. *Essays*, p. 191.
22. See especially his essay "Prophecy and Fulfilment," *Essays*, pp. 182–202.
23. *G. und V.*, Vol. I, pp. 313–336.
24. *Essays*, p. 208.
25. *ThNT*, Vol. I, p. 267.
26. *Essays*, p. 208.
27. *G. und V.*, Vol. I, p. 319.
28. *Ibid.*, p. 321.
29. *Ibid.*, pp. 323–324.
30. *Ibid.*, p. 319.
31. *Ibid.*, p. 336.
32. Jaspers and Bultmann, *Myth and Christianity*, p. 67.
33. *Ibid.*

34. Replying to Jaspers, Bultmann affirms that "as a Christian theologian I assert the absoluteness of the Christian revelation. . . . Wherever a revealed faith speaks it asserts, and must assert, the absoluteness of its revelation. . . . Everyone is free to regard such a revealed faith as absurd. But a man who does should not talk about revelation" (*ibid.*, pp. 67–68).

35. *Ibid.*, p. 68.

36. *Ibid.*, p. 69; cf. *E & F*, pp. 85–86.

37. *Essays*, p. 118.

38. *JC & M*, pp. 81–82.

39. *K & M*, p. 117.

40. In Kegley, ed., *op. cit.*, p. 261.

41. As he points out in *JC & M*, p. 71.

42. "The Question of Natural Revelation," *Essays*, pp. 90 ff.

43. See, e.g., *Essays*, p. 105.

44. *Ibid.*, p. 98.

45. *Ibid.*, p. 112.

46. See earlier, Chapter 4, n. 18.

47. *JC & M*, p. 69

48. *E & F*, p. 209.

49. "The Meaning of the Christian Faith in Creation," *E & F*, p. 206.

50. *Ibid.*, pp. 220–221.

51. "Faith in God the Creator" (1934); "The Meaning of the Christian Faith in Creation" (1936). Both are translated by Ogden in *E & F*.

52. *E & F*, p. 182.

6. God's Act in Jesus Christ

1. *K & M*, pp. 14–15, 23.
2. In Kegley, ed., *op. cit.*, pp. 274–275; cf. *Essays*, p. 85.
3. *K & M*, p. 202.
4. *Essays*, p. 286.
5. *Ibid.*, p. 280.
6. *Ibid.*, p. 286.
7. *Ibid.*, pp. 280–281.
8. *Ibid.*, p. 287.
9. *K & M*, p. 209, n. 1.
10. *Essays*, p. 16.

11. *Ibid.*, pp. 273 ff.

12. *Ibid.*, p. 287.

13. Barth, *Church Dogmatics*, ed. by G. W. Bromiley and T. F. Torrance (Charles Scribner's Sons, 1956), IV/1, p. 767.

14. Robert Cushman, "Is the Incarnation a Symbol?" *Theology Today*, Vol. 15 (1958), p. 177.

15. *Essays*, p. 286; cf. *K & M*, p. 209.

16. *Myth and Christianity*, p. 69; cf. *K & M*, p. 110.

17. *ThNT*, Vol. I, p. 302.

18. *JC & M*, pp. 78–79.

19. *K & M*, p. 209.

20. Barth, *Church Dogmatics*, IV/1, p. 767.

21. *K & M*, p. 115.

22. Macquarrie, *The Scope of Demythologizing*, pp. 29 ff.

23. Barth, *Rudolf Bultmann, ein Versuch*, p. 24.

24. Markus Barth, "Introduction to Demythologizing," *Journal of Religion*, Vol. 37 (July, 1957), p. 115.

25. Macquarrie, *An Existentialist Theology*, p. 243.

26. Fritz Buri, *Kerygma und Mythos*, Vol. II, pp. 85–101.

27. Schubert M. Ogden, "Bultmann's Project of Demythologizing and the Problem of Philosophy and Theology," *Journal of Religion*, Vol. 37 (1957), pp. 156 ff.

28. *Ibid.* This is also one of the main conclusions of Ogden's *Christ Without Myth* (Harper & Brothers, 1961), in which he denies Bultmann's contention that the transition from inauthentic to authentic existence can be described by philosophers but is effected only through the saving act of God in history.

29. In the above works, through numerous articles echoing his basic point of departure from Bultmann, and in a fuller account of his dependence on Whitehead and Hartshorne in *The Reality of God* (Harper & Row, Publishers, Inc., 1966).

30. *K & M*, p. 10.

31. *Ibid.*, p. 197.

32. Heinrich Ott, *op. cit.*, pp. 94–95, makes this point clear when he says: "Bultmann is not being inconsistent when he retains the once-for-all event of Christ because this event was the starting-point for the whole project of demythologizing which cannot be understood apart from this."

33. Henderson, *op. cit.*, p. 17.

34. *Christ Without Myth*, p. 112.

35. *Ibid.* In an article on "The Alleged Structural Inconsistency in Bultmann" (*Journal of Religion,* Vol. 44 [1964], pp. 193 ff.), Thomas Oden lets Ogden off too lightly at this point. He queries Ogden's use of the term *historisch* in the quoted description of Bultmann's view, but does not press the issue.

36. Ogden, "Bultmann's Project," *loc. cit.*, p. 168.

37. *Essays,* p. 288.

38. *K & M,* p. 107.

39. Macquarrie, *An Existentialist Theology,* p. 243.

40. Macquarrie, *The Scope of Demythologizing,* pp. 11 ff.

41. *K & M,* p. 110.

42. In Kegley, ed., *op. cit.*, p. 274.

43. *ThNT,* Vol. I, p. 26.

44. G. *und* V., Vol. I, p. 208.

45. *Essays,* p. 286.

46. H. P. Owen, *Revelation and Existence* (Cardiff: University of Wales, 1957), makes this charge, especially on p. 34.

47. *ThNT,* Vol. II, p. 66.

48. Jaspers and Bultmann, *Myth and Christianity,* p. 68.

49. Except that it began with him in the minimal sense that he serves as the prerequisite subject for preaching.

50. James M. Robinson, in his *New Quest of the Historical Jesus* (London: SCM Press, Ltd., 1959), discusses some of these.

51. In a lecture delivered at the Heidelberg Academy of Sciences, later published in translation in Braaten and Harrisville, eds., *The Historical Jesus and the Kerygmatic Christ.*

52. *Ibid.*, p. 20.

53. Seen particularly in his essay on "The New Approach to the Synoptic Problem," *E & F,* pp. 35 ff.

54. "The Primitive Christian Kerygma" in Braaten and Harrisville, eds., *op. cit.*, pp. 24–25.

55. Gogarten, *op. cit.*, p. 70.

56. *Ibid.*

57. F. Gogarten, "The Unity of History," *Theology Today,* Vol. 15 (July, 1958), p. 204.

58. *ThNT,* Vol. II, pp. 124 ff.

59. *Ibid.*, p. 71.

60. In an article on "The Study of the Synoptic Gospels" in *Form Criticism: A New Method of New Testament Research,* ed. by F. C. Grant (Willett Clark & Co., 1934).

61. *Ibid.*, p. 71.
62. McIntyre, *op. cit.*, p. 47.
63. *ThNT*, Vol. II, p. 123.
64. *Ibid.*, p. 48.

7. Man and His Existence

1. *JC & M*, p. 69.
2. *Ibid.*; cf. *K & M*, Vol. I, p. 39; *Jesus and the Word*, p. 158; *Primitive Christianity*, p. 18.
3. *ThNT*, Vol. II, p. 191.
4. *Essays*, pp. 83–84.
5. *G. und V.*, Vol. I, p. 324; cf. *Essays*, pp. 72, 78, 124–125, 224; *JC & M*, p. 30.
6. "Humanism and Christianity," *Journal of Religion*, Vol. 32 (1952), p. 83.
7. *H & E*, p. 44.
8. *Primitive Christianity*, pp. 166–167.
9. Just as my exposition in this section makes use of Macquarrie's lucid and convincing comparison of Bultmann and Heidegger in *An Existentialist Theology*.
10. *ThNT*, Vol. I, p. 196.
11. Macquarrie, *An Existentialist Theology*, p. 101.
12. *ThNT*, Vol. I, pp. 197–198.
13. *Ibid.*, p. 255.
14. *K & M*, p. 18.
15. Macquarrie, *An Existentialist Theology*, p. 104.
16. *ThNT*, Vol. I, p. 239.
17. Macquarrie, *An Existentialist Theology*, p. 160.
18. *Essays*, p. 84.
19. *Primitive Christianity*, p. 184.
20. *K & M*, p. 27.
21. *H & E*, pp. 150–151.
22. *K & M*, p. 31.
23. *Ibid.*, p. 32.
24. *ThNT*, Vol. I, pp. 289–290.
25. *Ibid.*, p. 290.
26. *Jesus and the Word*, p. 201.
27. *Essays*, p. 85.
28. *ThNT*, Vol. I, p. 284.

29. *K & M*, pp. 21–22; cf. *ibid.*, p. 121; *Essays*, p. 62; *Primitive Christianity*, p. 204.

30. *K & M*, p. 107.

31. *ThNT*, Vol. II, p. 175; cf. pp. 150, 180, 185.

32. *Jesus and the Word*, p. 51.

33. In Kegley, ed., *op. cit.*, p. xxii.

34. Karl Löwith, *Meaning in History* (The University of Chicago Press, 1957), p. 253.

35. *ThNT*, Vol. II, p. 203.

36. *Essays*, p. 289; *ibid.*, pp. 78, 153 ff., 207, 302; *K & M*, p. 20.

37. *Essays*, p. 154.

38. Bultmann points out that "although formal obedience to the law as such is no radical obedience . . . of course true obedience can exist in fulfilment of the law" (*Jesus and the Word*, p. 92).

39. *Primitive Christianity*, p. 92.

40. Thomas C. Oden, *Radical Obedience: The Ethics of Rudolf Bultmann* (The Westminster Press, 1964).

41. *Ibid.*, p. 131.

42. *Ibid.*, p. 144.

43. Heinz Horst Schrey, "The Consequences of Bultmann's Theology for Ethics," in Kegley, ed., *op. cit.*, pp. 183 ff.

44. *Ibid.*, p. 200.

45. Hans Bolewski, "The Role of the Church in the Theology of Rudolf Bultmann," in Kegley, ed., *op. cit.*, pp. 153 ff.

46. *Primitive Christianity*, p. 205; cf. *Essays*, p. 204.

47. Bultmann, "The Primitive Christian Kerygma," in Braaten and Harrisville, eds., *op. cit.*, p. 41, n. 80.

48. *ThNT*, Vol. II, p. 113.

49. *Ibid.*, pp. 199–200.

50. *Ibid.*, p. 114.

51. Bolewski, *op. cit.*, p. 168.

52. *JC & M*, pp. 82–83.

53. *Primitive Christianity*, p. 205.

INDEX